You're the
Ref!

Also by **Wayne Stewart:**

Wayne Stewart

Foreword by
Raymond Berry

You're the
Ref!

**174 Scenarios to Test
Your Football Knowledge**
Second Edition

Skyhorse Publishing

Skyhorse Publishing books may be purchased in bulk at special discounts for sales promotion, corporate gifts, fund-raising, or educational purposes. Special editions can also be created to specifications. For details, contact the Special Sales Department, Skyhorse Publishing, 307 West 36th Street, 11th Floor, New York, NY 10018 or info@skyhorsepublishing.com.

Skyhorse® and Skyhorse Publishing® are registered trademarks of Skyhorse Publishing, Inc.®, a Delaware corporation.

Visit our website at www.skyhorsepublishing.com.

10 9 8 7 6 5 4 3 2 1

Library of Congress Cataloging-in-Publication Data is available on file.

Interior photos courtesy of AP Images
Cover photo credit Thinkstock

ISBN: 978-1-63450-349-5
Ebook ISBN 978-1-63450-900-8
Printed in China

As usual, to my family: Nancy, Sean, Scott, Rachel, and Nathan.

CONTENTS

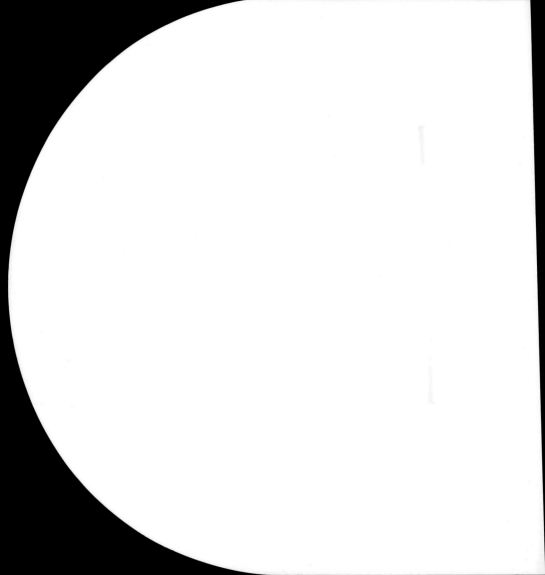

FOREWORD

By Raymond Berry

I was a split end for the Baltimore Colts from 1955 through the 1967 season. I spent quite a few years as an assistant coach for professional and college teams such as the Dallas Cowboys, the University of Arkansas, the Detroit Lions, the Cleveland Browns, and the New England Patriots. I also served as the head coach of the Patriots from 1984 through 1989. I played in three NFL championship games, including the classic sudden death game we won over the New York Giants in 1958—the one still called The Greatest Game Ever Played—and I coached the Patriots in the 1984 Super Bowl. Even now in retirement I stay connected to the game as a spectator.

I think, in a lot of ways, referees have an impossible job, so I've always been sympathetic to them. My dad was a Texas high school football coach so I grew up around the game. I was on the sidelines from the time I was eight years old, and somewhere along the way I realized how difficult their job is. My dad wasn't argumentative with refs, and I took that same approach as a player and as a coach. I never tried to "work" the officials because, for one thing, I realized that they weren't going to be perfect, that they're going to make mistakes.

YOU'RE THE REF!

When I coached the Patriots, I made it a point to teach my players to respect the referees. You figure that in the long run they'll make mistakes for you as well as making them against you. It all balances out eventually.

Plus, they tend to be pretty tolerant about things like ejecting players from the game. They don't do that lightly. All in all, referees are quite competent.

Actually, what I get most upset about relating to NFL rules isn't with the officiating, but it's with some rule changes made by the NFL, mainly the ones they've come up with to boost offenses. Referees simply have to call what they're told to call, and to ignore certain things. For example, the philosophy of what is considered to be holding nowadays is coming from the owners. They run the league and they set policy, so the game is going to be the way they want it.

They want to create offense. They want points put up on the board. So they turn a blind eye toward offensive linemen holding because that gives the quarterback more time to throw and gives the running backs bigger holes to run through.

I don't remember the names of too many referees, but a guy named Ron Gibbs comes to my mind as one of the best. He worked our 1958 championship game versus the New York Giants and he was so multi-talented; he even worked basketball games, including the NCAA title game in 1950.

In any case, this book will give you the opportunity to try to be a good ref, maybe a modern-day Gibbs. Your knowledge on many rules and situations that pop up in this great game will be tested. So, whether you may like a rule or not, you, as a football referee (for this book's purposes, at least), will have to get ready to blow your whistle and make the calls.

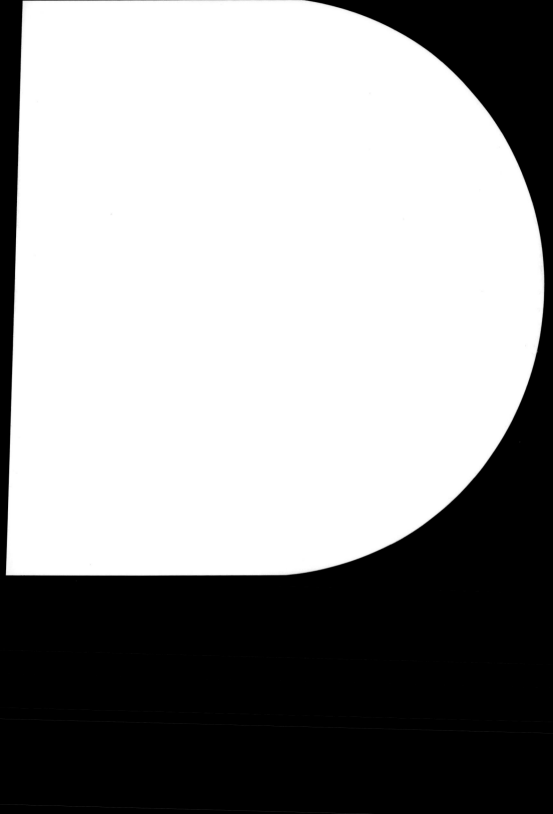

SUPER BOWL XLI

INTRODUCTION

On September 17, 1920, the American Professional Football Association, a forerunner to the NFL, was founded in Canton, Ohio. A handful of investors met in Hay's Hupmobile (automobile) showroom and each man plunked down $100, enough to purchase a team. No one could imagine the sophistication and complexity the game would eventually reach—not to mention the popularity and the profitability pro football would also attain.

For that matter, nothing about the game remained static, football has constantly been changing, and that fact is revealed vividly by taking a look at its ever-evolving rules. Compared to the Major League Baseball rule book, the NCAA and NFL rule books have an Etch A Sketch impermanence with new rules being added and old ones erased or revised frequently. In the early days of football, the rule books were as slim as a modern LED TV. By way of contrast, it's now unabridged dictionary–thick.

Over the years, the value of a field goal has changed from being four points, then five, back to four, and now, three points. As late as 1962 there was a rule in college football that stated a player could enter a game just once each quarter. It seems strange now; but if a player who was in the game at, say, the start of the second half left the game, he could not play again until the fourth quarter. Fortunately, over the years many such foolish rules fell by the wayside; but many, many new rules (some of which still seem confusing or odd) were written.

YOU'RE THE REF!

Some rules have come about due to unusual circumstances. Just as many a baseball park has a set of ground rules indigenous only to that venue, special rules had to be established when Chicago Stadium held football games. That facility, stated Pro Football Hall of Fame researcher Jon Kendle, was only sixty yards long from goal line to goal line. For a 1930 exhibition game held there between the Bears and the Cardinals, officials pushed the team with the ball back twenty yards after they returned each kickoff and another twenty yards after they crossed midfield—these actions made up for the short field, requiring each team to, in effect, travel a full hundred yards' worth of field. A punt that went out of the end zone meant the receiving team would take over at the fifteen-yard line; and if a punt hit a rafter, it was called a touchback, which also gave the receiving team the ball on their own fifteen.

Two years later, just ten years after the official inception of the NFL, a playoff game was played on that same field. The Chicago Bears and the Portsmouth Spartans, a franchise that would later switch cities and become the Detroit Lions, had finished their schedule tied for first place that necessitated an NFL first, a one-game playoff to determine the champs. The teams were forced to play indoors due to a blizzard that had struck the very Windy City with the force of a legion of blitzing linebackers.

The site chosen for the all-important game was Chicago Stadium with its short field that was also narrower than normal. The width of the field was so small "the sidelines butted up against the stands."

Faced with the problem of playing on that field, officials made the teams kick off from the ten-yard line. While details of games held in Chicago

Stadium are a bit hazy and conflicting reports exist, the fact is that this sports site did force special rules to be drawn up.

Many football rules were added with players' protection in mind—getting rid of dangerous formations such as the flying wedge was an early example of such a change. The game today is not nearly as rough and tumble—and lethal—as it once was. In the early days of the twentieth century, as many as a reported thirty-three players would die in a given football season. In that era the carnage on the gridiron was so fierce President Theodore Roosevelt declared that if action wasn't taken to improve the barbaric conditions, he would ban football altogether.

Further, at one time a man lugging the football was not considered to be downed when he was merely knocked to the ground. The definition of what constituted a tackle that would result in a dead ball was once stricter, and therefore violence-encouraging, than what it currently is, and "piling on" almost seemed to be a requirement to ensure a play would be whistled dead. Sometimes when a ballcarrier was lying on the ground but not officially down, a second tackler might come along and pounce on the vulnerable runner. Likewise, at times a ballcarrier who would be considered to be down by today's rules could spring back off the turf and continue his run if he wasn't deemed to be secured by the defense.

Research done by Jon Kendle revealed that in the 1921 Spalding Official Football Guide, one rule (Rule VI, Section 13, [a]), regarding when the ball was considered to be down, stated, among other things, that a player with the ball would be down when he is out of bounds, has his forward progress stopped, "or when any portion of his person except his hands or feet, touch the ground *while he is in the grasp of an opponent* [Italics added]."

In a 2011 e-mail, Kendle added, "By 1932 there was a provision to the rule and 'while he is in the grasp of an opponent' was taken out. Since the NFL created their own rule book in 1933, that change did not apply to them and they continued to use the 'while in the grasp of an opponent' phrase. In 1948 [the NFL] added 'irrespective of the grasp being broken.'

"It wasn't until 1956 that the NFL stated the ball is dead when 'a runner . . . is contacted by a defensive player and he touches the ground with any part of his body except his hands or feet.'" At such a point, the ball would instantly be declared dead.

In a 1979 interview, the brutality of the game was once more addressed and analyzed. Hard-hitting Dallas defensive back Cliff Harris stated, "If you have a chance to go for the interception or the hit, go for the hit. It makes a more lasting impression." Jack "the Assassin" Tatum of the notorious Oakland Raiders added, "To be a good safety, you have to be smart and something of a maniac," and said that the wicked hits he delivered to receivers was "the penalty for catching a pass." Much of the vicious contact (but certainly not all of it) has been eliminated from the pro game due to changes to the rule book.

Perhaps Jack Lambert was correct when he said rule changes, especially those to protect quarterbacks resulted in the "sissification," to coin a term, of the game; or, as he put it, quarterbacks ought to be outfitted with skirts. Decades later, after still more rules came about to guard quarterbacks, John Elway, himself a Hall of Fame quarterback, stated that while he used to detest Lambert's famous comment, he has since come to agree with the former Steelers star. In fact, he said that nowadays, "they should put them in ballerina outfits."

In October 2009, defensive end Corey Williams was hit with an unnecessary roughness penalty when he crashed on top of Buffalo signal caller Trent Edwards in the end zone. Williams recounted how the ref explained to him, "You drove him into the ground and landed on him." Williams countered by saying, "Where else am I going to land?" He then succinctly added, "It's football. I can tell it's an offensive game. They protect the quarterbacks and I understand that." Still, he finished by arguing that quarterbacks are nonetheless supposed to be football players. "That guy puts his uniform on just like the rest of us."

Those who favor the days of more physical contact and bone-rattling sacks almost expect that someday soon a rule will be enacted stating QBs must wear flags attached to a belt with Velcro; and defenders may not touch any part of the opposing quarterback but the flags—if they can pull one of the flags from him, then he is down; but any other contact would result in a fifteen-yard penalty, immediate ejection from the game, and a six-week suspension on top of that. Cowboys linebacker Bradie James put it more succinctly, "We're going to be playing flag football in about five years."

Clearly, though, rules to help players stay healthy, to avoid serious injury, have evolved just as the equipment of the game has—at one time a football helmet was so lacking in padding and protection it resembled a paper hat more than gladiator-like gear. In fact, the helmets could be folded up and placed in a player's back pocket. That truly was in a hungry era when the sport had a barroom brawl mentality about it and players held jobs in industries such as coal mining and steel manufacturing during off-seasons. Their football salaries were meager—the average salary for a player during the 1920–1932 era was around $100–$150 a game—unlike today's players who earn fortunes and certainly have no need to hold an additional job.

One source says that even as late as the late 1930s, there was no actual rule requiring NFL players to wear a helmet at all (another source states such a rule was not on the books until 1943); and Dick Plasman, a Chicago Bears end, is said to have been "the last NFL player to disdain a helmet, in 1940." As for college players, reference books indicate they didn't wear helmets until their game was "two decades into its existence." Yet another source states all players had to wear helmets for college play, but that only began being the case with the 1939 season. The point, nevertheless, remains—the early years of the game were rough and lacking in many rules to protect players.

It makes a person wonder how often a tackler led with his head back then. Were there considerable head-to-head barrages—which would have been legal as opposed to today's banned helmet-to-helmet illegal contact—and if so, how many fractured skulls ensued?

Some rules can be traced to innovative and/or punishing moves employed by certain players. The Oakland Raiders were said to be a team that looked for any advantage they could figuratively plunder. One rule change, the abolishment of the use of a substance called Stickum, which aided players in snagging a football, is traced back to a prime user of the sticky product,

Lester Hayes. This Oakland defensive back lathered the stuff to his hands just as spitball pitcher Gaylord Perry applied a dab of K-Y Jelly to his fingers and then to the baseball, with both men seeking an edge. Hayes's teammate Ted Hendricks commented, "You practically had to pry the ball loose from him whenever he got his hands on it." It was said that once Hayes had touched the pigskin, ball boys had to wipe it off before it could be put back into play. After the league banned Stickum in 1980, Hayes observed he was reduced to being "a mere mortal."

Men such as Ernie Stautner and Deacon Jones were so effective in using the head slap to an opponent's helmet, turning it into a mini-Liberty Bell and leaving that opponent in shock, a rule finally (in 1978) banned that move. To be clotheslined by six-foot-eight Doug Atkins (so strong he was capable of throwing a blocker at the quarterback) was to be on personal, excruciating terms with pain, so much so that the NFL also outlawed that tactic.

The NCAA not only creates new rules to make the game safer, but they also, said Mike Liner, who spent thirty-five years as a football official, "have their point of emphasis and code of conduct which they rewrite at the front of the rule book every year, and they emphasize to the officials that they want to protect [vulnerable] players."

On some occasions, rules came into being to make "the game easier for the average fan to follow," according to authors David S. Neft and Richard M. Cohen. For example, in the decade of the 1960s, officials' penalty flags, which had been white, were changed to gold, the color of the goalposts' uprights was changed to yellow, and a six-foot-wide white border was placed around the playing area in all NFL venues.

Enough background. It's time now for you to don your striped shirt because this book is designed to test your knowledge of the rules of college and pro football. You, in effect, become a referee (we'll use that term generically throughout the book instead of using terms such as back judge and umpire). Almost all of the plays you'll encounter, except where otherwise stated, are from real competition.

Admittedly, the degree of difficulty of the questions in this book varies greatly, with more than a handful of very easy as well as very difficult questions sprinkled throughout each of the book's sections. Depending upon how knowledgeable of a fan you are, some questions may offend you because they're no challenge at all and you'll breeze through those items. Others may seem unfair, too difficult to tackle—those may leave you feeling like a harried quarterback under the bombardment of a feral defense. Relax. Just try your best. You can always skip the easy ones and do a quarterback sneak (a sneak peek, that is) at the answers for those questions that seem to be a bit too challenging.

The book is organized by the types of plays that were run in the scenarios you're asked to explore. Although some of the penalties and situations described could perhaps have fit into several of the chapters, in a few cases I've placed scenarios wherever I felt they best fit.

So dig in, whet your football appetite, wet your referee's whistle, and prepare to toss your penalty marker as you make the call.

TAKE TO THE AIR: THE PASSING GAME

(1) Oregon was hosting Oregon State on December 3, 2009, with both teams nationally ranked (the Ducks were seventh in the nation and the Beavers were in the no. 16 slot) and both were vying for a trip to the Rose Bowl to face Ohio State. This was the 113th clash of the perennial rivals; but in this matchup, nicknamed the Civil War, a Rose Bowl bid was on the line.

In the first quarter, southpaw quarterback Sean Canfield threw a high pass to the five foot seven James Rodgers who soared to make the catch while also having to wrestle for the ball with John Boyett. Both men crashed to the ground while sharing possession of the football. Is this a completion or an interception?

Answer on page 33

(2) In college ball, if pass interference takes place, basically speaking, it usually costs the team on defense fifteen yards from the previous spot and an automatic first down. There are, of course, exceptions. For instance, as former college and current high school official Chuck

AARON RODGERS

Braun pointed out, "In college if the spot of the interference is *less* than 15 yards from the previous spot, the ball is placed at the spot of the interference with an automatic first down." In short, he added, "The maximum distance penalty in college is 15 yards, but it could be less." Also, if interference occurs in the end zone, the ball is spotted on the two-yard line with an automatic first down.

This is a penalty some fans feel is ludicrous—after all, if a defender gets burned by a receiver so badly, a long touchdown catch seems imminent. The player who just became "toast" will, in effect, be rewarded by interfering with the receiver (he can virtually mug the player) in that his infraction will hurt his team to the tune of those fifteen yards, but that's a whole lot better than surrendering a quick six points. In the most extreme situation, a defender could nullify a potential ninety-nine-yard TD toss and give the offense a mere fifteen yards instead by committing an illegal act.

What are, as stated above for the college game, the basic rules regarding defensive pass interference in the NFL?

Answer on page 33

(3) Picture Penn State's all-time leading rusher Evan Royster rolling out of the backfield for a swing pass, but he is interfered with behind the line of scrimmage. What's your call?

Answer on page 35

11

(4) In NFL play, a defensive end, anticipating the snap, trying to get some impetus behind his bull rush of the quarterback in an obvious passing situation, takes a step forward before the snap is made. He gets caught in the neutral zone just as ball is then snapped. The referee allows the play to continue, giving a free shot to the QB. That is, the quarterback could try to throw a bomb, realizing that even if it is intercepted, the penalty will wipe out the pick and give the offense five yards for the infraction. Was the official correct in letting the play (probably a pass play) continue?

Answer on page 36

(5) An imaginary situation from 2010 has New York quarterback Eli Manning driving the Giants down to the Washington Redskins eighteen-yard line. He decides to throw a pass to Mario Manningham who, at first, appears to be wide open. However, defensive back Kareem Moore picks off the pass while standing about eight yards deep into the end zone and elects to run it out. Then, seeing that his end of the field is infested with Giants, he realizes it would be more profitable for his Skins if he simply downs the ball.

Now, because he began to run the ball toward the goal line, is he committed to continue running—if he stops and takes a knee, could this actually result in a safety once the defense gets to him?

Answer on page 36

6 Follow-up question: what if the defensive back who came up with the interception had crossed the plane of the end zone on his run back *then* decided to reenter the end zone and down the ball. He is then tackled in the end zone. Is it a safety, or was his move of reentering the end zone for a touchback within the rules, permitting his team to take over at the twenty-yard line?

Answer on page 36

7 Nowadays in college football, a runner is declared to be down once a part of his body, such as, but not confined solely to, a knee has touched the turf. What if a receiver—let's just say, it's Noel Devine—slipped while running his route out of the backfield and is actually lying on the ground as he makes a catch. Is this, in fact, a catch and the play is over—he's down and can't advance the ball—or because he was down when he made the grab, is the pass ruled an incompletion?

Answer on page 37

8 The Pittsburgh Panthers were home to the Syracuse Orangemen on the November 14, 2009, already leading comfortably, 27–3, late in the third stanza. Pitt's quarterback, Bill Stull, rolled out and lofted a high pass that was picked by Syracuse's Phil Thomas. He came up with a nifty return; but after being tackled, he noticed the field was littered with flags. There were three penalties on the same play.

The first penalty was by an Orangeman defensive back, Phillip Thomas, who had been guilty of holding an eligible receiver, doing so before the interception occurred. The next two took place after the interception and were both committed by the same Syracuse player, Arthur Jones. How did all this pan out?

Answer on page 37

(9) Imagine an NFL quarterback pitches the ball to his halfback, a few yards behind him. The QB then rolls out and runs a pass pattern. He's wide open—can the running back now throw a forward pass to the QB? Is he an eligible receiver or not?

Answer on page 37

(10) In 2009 Colorado visited Darrell K. Royal–Texas Memorial Stadium in Austin, Texas, to take on the Longhorns. With traditions such as the Hook 'em Horns signals on display throughout the stands, the singing of "The Eyes of Texas" the blasting of Smokey the Cannon, the booming sound of five-hundred-pound Big Bertha, the world's largest bass drum, and the omnipresence of longhorn mascot Bevo XIV, pageantry and tradition were on display.

In the final quarter, Colorado was desperately trying to mount a comeback from a ten-point deficit, 24–14. Texas, number two in the country at that point (October 10), pinned the Buffaloes into a third-and-five situation with just under thirteen minutes to play. The game's starting quarterback, Cody Hawkins, the son of Colorado's head coach, Dan, was on the bench by this point, putting the come-back onus on Tyler Hansen.

Hansen dropped back and was under siege by a heavy Texas rush (led by Roddrick Muckelroy), one so fierce he was forced out of the pocket where he weakly unleashed the ball that didn't even travel back to the line of scrimmage. Is this a legal play, or did flags fly?

Answer on page 37

11   Let's say wide receiver Mike Williams of the Tampa Bay Buccaneers is in the end zone when his quarterback, Josh Freeman, peppers the ball toward him. Williams catches it while his entire body, except his hands, is in the end zone. We'll say his hands were extended back into the field of play to snag the ball. Williams was then immediately shoved out of bounds by Cincinnati Bengals defensive back Leon Hall, just as he made the catch. Is this a score?

Answer on page 38

12   Imagine a crisp pass is intended for running back Michael Turner circling out of the Atlanta backfield on a short route in 2010. The football skims off his fingertips and takes off down field where Roddy White, his teammate, is able to snatch it. Is this a legal catch?

Answer on page 38

15

(13) Navy traveled to Cleveland where they played the Ohio State Buckeyes on the opening weekend of the 2009 NCAA season. Despite being miles away from the Columbus campus, the Buckeye motif was prevalent in the northeast Ohio late summer air: Mascot Brutus Buckeye was on hand, OSU players were keyed up to earn more Buckeye leaf decals for their helmets, and of course, the marching band had made the trip, anxious once more for the drum major of The Best Damn Band in the Land to guide a sousaphone player to the spot where he would dot the *i* in *Ohio* as they performed the Script Ohio formation on the field pre-game (a tradition dating back to 1936).

Navy's offense had led the entire nation in rushing over the previous four seasons, and their triple option offense was one Jim Tressel's team had never before faced. Some observers felt the game just might turn out to be an interesting one.

They proved to be correct. OSU gave up 186 yards to the Navy ground game, almost twice as many yards as they had permitted on average per game over the previous season.

Ohio State entered the final quarter with a seemingly safe fifteen-point spread over Navy. After scoring a touchdown, the Midshipmen's second of the quarter, at the 2:23 mark of the fourth quarter to draw within two points of the highly favored Buckeyes, 29–27, Navy went for a two-point conversion. Their quarterback Ricky

Dobbs faded back and threw a pass; but it was picked off by Brian Rolle, a junior middle linebacker. He was off and streaking, on a roll, to use a pun, with Dobbs in pursuit down the sideline, representing the last chance to stop Rolle. After Dobbs was finally outdistanced, Rolle finished his interception return of 99 yards, tumbling into the Midshipmen end zone, triggering raucous cheering and prompting Rolle to confess that he "was looking for an oxygen tank."

As an official working that game, what would you have ruled on this play, and what about if this unusual event took place in the NFL?

Answer on page 38

(14) Related (trick?) question: how much time ticked off the clock during this play?

Answer on page 39

(15) Here's an easy question. Picture this imaginary situation from 2010—Houston Texan quarterback Matt Schaub takes the snap and hands the ball off to Arian Foster who plunges ahead, nearly into the pile of linemen directly ahead of him; but at the last moment, he spins and laterals the ball back to Schaub who then throws a forward pass, completing it for a thirty-five-yard gain to Kevin Walter. Should a penalty marker be thrown on this trick play?

Answer on page 39

(16) Dan Reeves was a fine running back with the Dallas Cowboys long before he became a head coach in the NFL. As the leader of the Denver Broncos for an even dozen seasons, he won three AFC Championships (and added an NFC title later with Atlanta), captured six of his seven Division Championships, and was victorious 110 times versus 73 losses, good for a .601 winning percentage.

As a player, he excelled at the halfback option, a play in which the runner has the choice of either passing the ball or tucking it under his arm and carrying out a run.

In this scenario, Reeves decides to pull up and heave a pass on a fly pattern to the human bullet Bobby Hayes, a man who could outrun a cheetah. Reeves is hit a bit late, clearly at least a second or so after he had already released the ball. Is he protected by the rules as if he were the team's quarterback?

Answer on page 40

(17) Related item: Does a running back such as Reeves, or for that matter, a receiver who throws the ball have to obey all the rules that pertain to a quarterback such as intentional grounding of the football?

Answer on page 40

(18) Say quarterback Matt Cassel of the Kansas City Chiefs fades into his own end zone where he is under siege from a ferocious bull rush by defensive end Robert Mathis of the Indianapolis Colts. If Cassel gets sacked in end zone, it is, of course, a safety and two points for the Colts. However, what would happen if one of his offensive linemen, recognizing Cassel was in deep trouble, decides he must protect his quarterback at all costs even if it means not obeying the rules? So to prevent the safety, he holds Mathis who is about five yards deep into the end zone himself. How would a ref handle this situation?

Answer on page 40

(19) Say Boston College is taking on the Clemson Tigers in this next imaginary situation, and Clemson quarterback Kyle Parker, son of former NFL receiver Carl Parker, is in the shotgun formation. The ball is snapped low but Parker is able to haul it in by kneeling down for the ball. If his knee touches the turf while he has possession of the ball, is he instantly down, or is there a rule that makes such a play an exemption to the normal college rule about an offensive player being down when he touches the ground with his knee?

Answer on page 42

(20) Here's a tie-in to an earlier question concerning the rules of the college ranks—this one is for beginners only. Reggie Wayne of the Colts is running his route when he stumbles and sprawls to the grass fifteen yards from the line of scrimmage. Even though his knees have

touched the ground and he is, in fact, still lying on the ground, his stellar quarterback Peyton Manning fires the ball his way; and Wayne hauls it in.

The questions in this made-up situation are these: Does Wayne get credit for a catch and the positive yardage, or since he's down, is he also out—that is to say, is the catch illegal and nullified? If it's a legal catch, is the play over once he touched the ball while also being in contact with the ground?

Answer on page 43

(21) Here's another very easy one, even for a casual fan. Let's just say that Green Bay running back Brandon Jackson dashes across the line of scrimmage and then quickly, before he can become engaged by the defense, retreats to a point just behind that line of demarcation. Suddenly he spots a wide open receiver, and he hurls the ball for a huge gain. Is this a legal maneuver?

Answer on page 43

(22) Let's travel back in time to 1981. Cincinnati's quarterback Ken Anderson backpedals to pass, stays in the pocket, then throws a shovel pass to running back Pete Johnson who is a few yards in front of him. Is an underhand or a side-armed forward pass legal?

Answer on page 43

TAKE TO THE AIR: THE PASSING GAME

(23) With the score tied at 3–3 early in the second quarter of the NFL playoff game between the Indianapolis Colts and the Baltimore Ravens on January 16, 2010, the Colts had the ball at the Ravens' thirty-nine-yard line. Manning faded to pass and threw a ball that never got very far as it was quickly batted away by Baltimore's Clint Session. It flew, not unlike a jump ball in the NBA, up for grabs.

Colts' running back Joseph Addai, hungry for the football, propelled himself toward it, taking on the appearance of a human cannonball, and gobbled it up in midair, apparently preventing Ravens' Dannell Ellerbe from picking off the pass. Addai came down with the ball and a meager two-yard gain. Far more vital to the Colts' cause, though, his actions allowed Indianapolis to maintain possession of the football—or did he? Can an offensive player catch a deflected pass as described here?

Answer on page 43

(24) Here's a twist on the previous question. In this instance, the year is 1972; and during an NFL game, just as the football was about to reach a receiver, the nearest defensive back on the scene converged, but in this scenario he does *not* make contact with the ball (more on that later). Imagine the ball hit off the receiver who was struck by the DB a split second after touching the football; and the ball then ricocheted back toward the line of scrimmage where a running back, who had circled out of the backfield on his pass route, was standing. Fortuitously, the ball rebounded directly to him; he pulls the ball in and darts for a score. Count it or not?

Answer on page 43

(25) On September 19, 2009, early in the NCAA schedule, the Washington Huskies were at home to the mighty (then ranked third in the nation) USC Trojans in Seattle, Washington.

Coming into the game, the Trojans knew they'd be without their starting quarterback Matt Barkley who was coming off a glistening showing the week before in an 18–15 win over Ohio State. The nineteen-year-old freshman was sidelined, though, by a sore shoulder.

In the early part of the fourth quarter, Washington, on a ten-game losing streak in Pac-10 encounters, felt fairly good about their chances for an upset—the weekend before, they had halted a fifteen-game losing string by topping Idaho, and they were currently playing USC toe to toe.

On a first-and-ten situation, Huskies quarterback Jake Locker faded to pass; but after launching the football, it was deflected by six foot four linebacker Michael Morgan. The ball bounced back to Locker who then tried to bat the ball, volleyball-spike style, to the ground to avoid a potential interception. At that point the football struck Trojans' defensive end Wes Horton and bounded yet again, this time over to offensive lineman Ben Ossai, a 335-pounder who caught it well behind the line of scrimmage. He then lumbered for a few yards before being wrestled to the ground, winding up with a net loss of one yard that, nevertheless, put him in the books for having made a reception, a rare delicacy for offensive linemen.

Has anything illegal transpired here—would you have thrown your flag on the play?

Answer on page 46

(26) Follow-up item: if the circumstances from the above question changed a bit, would you still make the same call? Let's say that this time the football was not tipped but, due to a mix-up, the quarterback, scrambling for his life, thinks he has spotted his big tight end but instead mistakenly threw directly to an offensive lineman who managed to rumble into the end zone for an apparent touchdown. Would you let the six points stand?

Answer on page 47

(27) Another simple imaginary situation: T. J. Moe, a fine wide receiver for Missouri, catches a ball while he is in the air and is about a yard deep into the end zone. Now, an opposing cornerback belts him with the wild enthusiasm of a teenager playing Slug (or Punch) Bug, supplying

sufficient force to drive Moe back out of the end zone, back to about the one-yard line, ball still clutched to his body. Where is the ball spotted? What's your ruling on the play?

Answer on page 47

(28) The next question takes you back to the NFL title game of December 27, 1953, held between the Detroit Lions, the reigning league champs who had already captured the '53 Western Conference title, and the underdog Cleveland Browns who were the current Eastern Conference champions and who were trying to usurp the Lions' crown in Briggs Stadium located in the heart of the Motor City. Incidentally, formerly the two conferences were known as the National and the American conferences, respectively.

Be aware that this question requires you to carefully consider the time period involved and the rules that existed at that time.

At any rate, the game was, of course, a huge one and featured such luminaries as quarterback Otto Graham and Lou "the Toe" Groza for the Browns and quarterback Buddy Layne and Doak Walker for the Lions.

The Browns had won eleven straight games to open the season, losing only in their regular season finale. In the meantime, Detroit had gone 10–2.

In the first half, the Lions had the ball at about the Browns nineteen-yard line when the colorful and talented Layne pitched the ball to Walker who swept toward his right. Suddenly, he stopped short, ending his bid for a run, and threw cross field and hit none other than Layne who had swung out of the backfield and rolled out to the opposite side of the field from Walker.

Layne not only gathered in the swing pass at about the line of scrimmage, but he also rambled into the end zone. However, shortly thereafter, the refs made it clear the touchdown did not count. Exactly why was the score disallowed?

Answer on page 48

(29) The Chicago Bears were playing division rival Green Bay in 1986 when quarterback Jim McMahon threw an interception and began to stroll off the field. Before he could reach the sidelines, Charles Martin of the Packers shed a blocker, got to McMahon, slammed him to the ground, and then hovered over his supine body. Bears tackle Jim Covert bolted over to Martin and knocked him to the ground. How do you handle this, and what calls took place that day?

Answer on page 48

(30) Imagine Arizona has traveled to Penn State, a university nestled near Mount Nittany in Happy Valley. Say the year is 1999 and Consensus All-American linebacker La Var Arrington of Penn State (a school fittingly known as "Linebacker U" thanks to their twelve first team All-Americans at that position through the 2009 season) picks off a Wildcat pass at

his own three-yard line. His momentum carries him into the end zone where he is promptly tackled by the intended wide receiver. As the ref covering this play (which is similar to an earlier question you fielded), do you rule that the ball belongs to PSU on the interception at the three-yard line, at the twenty-yard line, ruling this is a touchback, or because he was nabbed in his team's end zone, is this a safety?

Answer on page 49

(31) On September 19, 2009, Texas took on Texas Tech in Austin. Long-horns' quarterback, the man with an ideal name for a Texas QB, Colt McCoy, hit his favorite target and close friend, Jordan Shipley, with a pass. Shipley, a receiver with hands like flypaper, then chugged forward a bit before he was jostled out of bounds by the defender. Should the clock be stopped or kept running after Shipley was forced beyond the sideline chalk?

Answer on page 50

(32) Under the rules of the NFL, can a team use a player other than a back or a receiver to run a pattern and catch a pass—or would that be considered an illegal receiver situation?

In other words, could a team line up a hulking defensive player as a tight end (or, for that matter, in the back field), or does his normal position and/or jersey number determine where he must play?

Answer on page 52

33 Imagine this play taking place in the year 2010 in the NFL: a wide receiver makes a catch in the end zone, comes down with both feet, but then, a second later, dropped the ball after his hand came down and the football then squirted loose. Is this a score or not?

Answer on page 55

34 This one takes us back to November 4, 1972. LSU, in their home stadium, known affectionately to their fans as Death Valley, was taking on Mississippi; and the game had wound down to the four-second mark in the fourth quarter. Quarterback Bert Jones took a deep drop of about ten yards, executed a pump fake, then threw an incomplete pass. Somehow, even after all of that activity had taken place, one second remained on the clock. The Jones pass simply *had* to have taken longer than four seconds. So was the game declared to be over or not?

Answer on page 56

35 During the December 16, 1945, NFL title game, won by the Cleveland Rams over the Redskins, the deciding play turned out to be an odd one. In the first quarter, Washington's quarterback Slingin' Sammy Baugh released a pass from his own end zone; and the ball, due to a strong wind, hit the goalpost. What was the ruling back then in a time when the goalpost's location was directly on the goal line (a new rule enacted in 1974 would move the posts to the rear of the end zones)?

Answer on page 57

(36) The Baltimore Ravens played host to the Steelers in December of 2008. Late in the first half, Baltimore drove to the Steelers' eight-yard line. Joe Flacco faked a quarterback sneak, then lobbed the ball high into the end zone where it ricocheted off the crossbar and deflected to Pittsburgh's Lawrence Timmons. Is this an interception or not?

Answer on page 57

(37) When Iowa played Penn State in late September 2009, the Hawkeye quarterback, Ricky Stanzi, hit Colin Sandeman with a pass that hit him near his chest, then bounced off him and toward the ground. Sandeman kicked the ball high in the air and then tried to secure it, but Nick Sukay picked it off. Is this situation similar to college basketball—was the kicking of the football an infraction, making the play dead; or did the interception give PSU the ball?

Answer on page 57

(38) In NFL action from 2008, Tennessee Titan Justin Gage was almost out of bounds when he made a circus catch, managed to keep the tiptoes of both feet in bounds, then had his heels come down on the chalk of the sidelines. Did the fact that the heels touched out of bounds matter or not?

Answer on page 57

39 Early on during a 1932 NFL playoff game between the Bears and the Portsmouth Spartans, both teams came to realize this one would be a low-scoring affair. In fact, it remained scoreless after three quarters. Then Canadian-born superstar Bronko Nagurski, who, at six feet two and listed between 217 and 235 pounds, was considered to be a bruising large fullback, took matters into his own meaty hands (when he was measured for his ring for being on an NFL title team, observers were astonished to see the ring size check in at 19 ½, said to be the largest recorded size for a player measured for the championship ring).

An interception and a ten-yard return by Chicago's Dick Nesbitt gave the Bears the ball on the Portsmouth thirteen-yard line. Two Nagurski carries moved the ball to the two-yard line. There, Nagurski took the ball, faded a few steps (say he was four yards deep into his backfield at this point), and threw a pass to another legend, Red Grange, for a touchdown.

Now, unless you're a true historian of the game, this is one question you will probably miss: according to the NFL rule book back then, why should the score *not* have been permitted, given that everything described above is correct?

Answer on page 57

40 Wide receiver Dave Smith of the Pittsburgh Steelers caught a pass during a Monday Night Football game versus the Chiefs in 1971. He took off for the goal line and would have scored except for one small detail—he spiked the ball on the three-yard line, a costly miscalculation.

29

This one is included here because it is such an interesting play, but it isn't a difficult one to figure out. What call did the refs make that day?

Answer on page 58

(41) On January 3, 2011, the Orange Bowl featured Stanford and Virginia Tech. Stanford had the ball on their own five-yard line late in the first quarter. Andrew Luck faded into his own end zone. There, under severe pressure, he dumped the ball off in an effort to avoid a safety. The ball was batted by Virginia Tech's Antoine Hopkins, then caught by Derek Hall who promptly fell to the ground in the end zone. What was the call here?

Answer on page 59

(42) The following day, Ohio State met Arkansas in the Sugar Bowl. D. J. Williams of Arkansas snared a pass from Ryan Mallett but was hit by Ross Homan, who was on the ground. Before Williams could be brought to the ground, he rolled over Homan. Only his wrist touched down as he stayed on his feet and scooted into the end zone. Is this a touchdown or not?

Answer on page 59

(43) Earlier in this chapter there was a question much like the following, but that situation pertained to college ball so here goes your new challenge. In the NFL, what happens when both a defender and a receiver appear to have possession of a pass, with both men having their arm(s) or hand(s)

wrapped around the ball? Do you award the ball to the offensive team or to the defensive team, or does another rule come into play here?

Answer on page 59

(44) Utah and Stanford played a game in 2014 that featured one of the oddest and most sudden turnarounds ever. The turnaround here involved a swing of twelve potential points in a matter of seconds. Utah wide receiver Kaelin Clay's name now belongs next to names such as "Wrong Way" Roy Riegels when it comes to making mental blunders. Here's exactly what happened.

Utah, ranked No. 17 in the country, led No. 4 Oregon, 7–0, and, even though the game had just entered the second quarter, Utah was smelling an upset. After hauling in a pass for what seemed like a relatively easy seventy-eight-yard touchdown, Clay dropped the ball before he crossed the goal line, doing so with a little flip of his wrist, providing fans with what he must have thought was a dramatic flair.

The television announcer bellowed, "Touchdown," and Utah players began to celebrate. Alert Oregon players didn't mope, though. After just a bit of confusion and a delay of a second or so, Oregon's Erick Dargan picked up the ball, then dropped it, but junior linebacker Joe Walker was also on the spot, scooping up the ball and rambling ninety-nine yards for six points.

With so many Utes far from the ball, celebrating, with an armada of blockers (six by one count) ahead of him, and with only one opponent in his way, Walker coasted into the end zone. What could have been a 14-0 game at that point was quickly turned into a 7–7 tie.

Your question, as the ball sat on the ground at the one-yard line, what signal did the officials give to indicate the ball was live?

Answer on page 60

 On the same play described above, Dargan actually picked up the ball *after* he had run a few steps off the playing field, and before he realized Utah had not scored. Should there be a penalty for him leaving the field then returning to it to gain possession of the football?

Answer on page 61

 Final question regarding this wild play: Is such a play reviewable under NCAA rules or not?

Answer on page 61

True or false—and be careful, as this question is a bit tricky (or picky): In order for a quarterback to avoid being called for intentional grounding on a pass to an area where there is no eligible receiver, the passer must be outside the tackle box when he makes his throw and the pass must go beyond the line of scrimmage.

Answer on page 61

ANSWERS

(1) This situation harkens to the old baseball expression "A tie goes to the runner," a saying that, by the way, is not true—umpires say there is no such thing as a tie, that a runner, even on the closest of bang-bang plays, is either safe or out. In this situation, though, there is a rule that states that if two men are grappling for the ball and both have control of it—a dual possession situation—then after all the jostling is over, the football is awarded to the offense.

Oregon went on to win a wild one on a 37–33 decision, hoisting their win-loss slate to 10–2, 8–1 in the conference, good enough to take home the Pac-10 championship, ending the USC stranglehold of seven seasons. Meanwhile, Rodgers went on to take second team honors as the all-purpose player on the AP All-American team that was selected in December 2009.

(2) In the NFL, the team on offense gets the ball at the spot of the infraction plus an automatic first down; so unlike in the college ranks, there is no maximum distance penalty on pass interference calls. Furthermore, if the interference occurs in the end zone, the offensive team is given a first down and the ball at the one-yard line. Without getting into rules that are more complex, these are the basics regarding pass interference.

33

DENARD
ROBINSON

Liner defended the college rule. "There are a couple of reasons they changed that [rule]. The way it was explained to me by our supervisor several years ago when they changed it is they want the penalty called. That very play you described, that's a game-changer. I mean, you just gave them 98 yards on your penalty.

"The official has got to say, 'Look, was that really bad enough to give them 98 yards?' But now you can say, 'That was pass interference; we're going to give them 15 and a first down.' You put the thing in per-spective. Let's make the penalty commensurate with the foul. That's the deal. You want the thing called and the way you make it called is you don't absolutely take the other team's head off. That call is like the death penalty. If you're on the jury and you're giving somebody 20 years or death, it's easier to give them 20 years—you're going to make that call, but it's hard to make the death penalty call."

3 Had Royster, who usurped Curt Warner in 2010 to become the top PSU runner of all time, been, say, a yard beyond the line, Penn State would have picked up a first down and fifteen yards from the pre-vious spot, that is, from the line of scrimmage. However, and this comes as a surprise to some fans, "You cannot have pass interference behind the line of scrimmage," said Liner. "Period."

"You can have holding that receiver back there, you can call that, which would be 10 yards from the previous spot and an automatic first down." To some extent, then, a receiver behind the line is fair game for the defense—within reason, of course. As Liner elaborated, "You can't do a personal foul. You know, you can't hit me in the head or spear me or slug me, that kind of stuff, but if you come in with your shoulder and knock me on my ass behind the line of scrimmage and you're a linebacker covering me and you catch me behind the line and you say, 'I'm supposed to be covering this guy. I think I'll knock his ass down so I don't have to worry about him catching the ball,' that's completely legal—even if the ball's in the air coming straight at him."

(4) Yes. As Ed Dohanos, a man who has officiated football at both the high school and college level, noted, "The defensive player can get back [onside] provided he didn't draw anybody [offside]." However, if he's still in the neutral zone as the ball is snapped, he is charged with a penalty, and the play does continue. This does, in fact, give the quarterback carte blanche to try any play "if he's alert to the situation."

(5) No, he is permitted to stop, reconsider the situation, then take a knee. The ball would go out to the twenty-yard-line.

(6) Such a move by the defensive back in question would result in a safety. Once he crossed the goal line, it was too late for him to go back into the end zone without risking being tackled there for a safety. So in this case, chalk up two points for making the tackle in the end zone and chalk up a huge faux pas for the defensive back.

(7) Easy question. It's a legal catch for Devine and the play is then dead.

(8) The hold stood as the only penalty that mattered, costing Syracuse ten yards and giving the Panthers an automatic first down. Pitt declined the other two penalties and maintained the football.

(9) Yes, a quarterback is considered to be an eligible receiver.

(10) In college football, Hansen's pass, at first blush, may appear to have been legal—he is certainly permitted to sling the ball away. However, because he was flushed out of the pocket and outside the tackle box, in order to avoid a rules violation, he had to have his pass reach the line of scrimmage or go beyond it. Because his throw didn't go that far due to the fact that he couldn't get anything on the ball, he was guilty of committing a spot foul that entailed a loss of down.

The infraction became an important play in the contest; due to the penalty, which set Colorado back deeply, they were faced with a fourth and twenty. The Buffaloes were forced to punt and Matthew DiLallo's kick to Jordan Shipley (who added over a hundred yards receiving that day) was returned for a seventy-four-yard score, thanks to some nifty moves and a burst of speed, to crack the game wide open.

The Longhorns' special teams scored twice in the half, and Coach Mack Brown's Texas squad coasted to a 38–14 win to remain undefeated on the year at 5–0.

Incidentally, Brown went into the year with nineteen consecutive winning seasons, second best among active coaches and trailing only the legendary Bobby Bowden. He had also strung together seventeen straight bowl appearances, a feat that also trailed only Bowden among active coaches going into the 2009 campaign.

(11) No, this is not a touchdown. The rule about scoring a touchdown is as simple as it is rigid—the ball must break the plane of the end zone or it's not a TD. In this case, the hands, with the ball in them, did not penetrate the end zone.

(12) Years ago such a play, involving a deflection that went directly from one offensive player to another, was illegal—it was a catch if the ball had hit an intended receiver, hit off a defender first, and *then* was seized by a member of the offensive team—but that rule went by the board quite some time ago. In this scenario, credit White with a catch.

(13) In college football, the team running back the interception on a two-point conversion attempt is rewarded with two points of their own.

So after the score by Rolle, Ohio State not only took a four-point lead, but Navy also had to kick off to them; and even if Navy quickly managed to get the ball back, a field goal would not have been good enough to tie the Buckeyes. Thus, they would have had to regain the football, either via an onside kick or by playing tough defense, and still would have been forced to score a TD on the Ohio State D. They couldn't do it—the Buckeyes recovered an onside kick, and it was all over. Navy's bid for a stunning upset fell short with the score of 31–27 holding up.

Under NFL rules, the team on defense cannot score during a kick or two-point conversion attempt.

Trivia item: during the first few days of the New Year in 1945, many troops stationed around the globe during World War II staged their version of Army-Navy bowl games, giving them unique names. For example, in Florence, Italy, the game was called the Spaghetti Bowl; in Hawaii it was the Poi Bowl (held in a venue known as the Termite Palace); and in Dijon, France, the Mustard Bowl was played.

(14) None. The clock does not start on either a one-point kick or a two-point conversion attempt.

(15) No, it's a perfectly legal play.

(16) Yes, any player striking a passer belatedly will be hit with a penalty—after all, the infraction is labeled "roughing the passer," not roughing the quarterback.

(17) Sure, after all there is no logical reason why he should be exempt from such rules.

(18) Holding behind the goal line is an automatic safety. If a lineman is correct that his quarterback is doomed and is about to get sacked, he might figure, "Why not try to hold, but try to be surreptitious, as subtle about it if feasible." If he isn't spotted by an official, then he could indeed save his team two points.

By the way, don't believe everything television announcers tell you about holding. How many times have you heard it said that refs could call holding on virtually every single play? Former college line judge Mike Liner says that's simply not so. "There are a lot of plays you couldn't call holding on. There are a lot of plays where you probably could make a case for it, but I don't believe that people that watch the game understand the game enough to understand what holding is. You gotta have another verb to go with holding. If a guy says I'm holding, then the question is how am I holding you? Did I yank you? Did I grasp you, did I pull you, did I tug you, did I twist you?

"When I was officiating in the Big 12 and we wrote up our penalty reports after the game, and you had a holding call during that game, you had to describe it, 'Number 76 grabbed number 92 and yanked him by the left arm,' or twisted him, or tackled him. The officials were required to add a descriptive verb beyond simply saying there was holding on the play or you didn't have anything. So if anybody looked at the film and they saw number 76 on number 92, and they didn't see number 92 get yanked or grasped or some other [such] action there, then you don't have holding. Yeah, he may have had a hold of his jersey, but unless you see some other verb, [there's no holding]."

Tim Millis, a former NFL official who also once worked in the Big 12, elaborated on what Liner said, "I used to say as the Big 12 supervisor, you've got to have some other verb associated with that restriction. The five common ones used to describe a material restriction are a grab, a hook, a takedown, a jerk, a pull, or a turn. All of these verbs are evidence of some restriction.

"The official also looks to what happens to the defender to determine the restriction. For example, does his shoulder dip, is he turned away from the direction he's heading, is he pulled to or toward the ground, are his feet 'taken away' after he has beat the blocker?"

Therefore, Millis summarized, "You couldn't call it on every play the way they define it. You have to have some type of restriction of movement on the defensive player—you have to restrict that player's movement and it goes without saying that it's got to be somewhere that's relevant and has a material effect on the play." In other words, normally, "There has to be a material restriction at the point of the attack or a flagrant hold somewhere away from the point of attack that could cause retaliation."

(19) The play is over and the team will lose some serious yardage. There is no clemency, no break given here for a botched play. This can be a split-second call, though, not as easy to make as it may sound. Liner said, "It's a pretty tough call. The referee has got to be on his game. As soon as he sees a low snap, he's got to be ready for those things to happen because they can happen in a flash of an eye."

Next is a spin-off question. What about a punter? What if he had to drop down to his knee to take a low snap—is he down, or is this type of play an exception to the usual rule?

The rule also holds true for a punter. If he touches the ground (probably with a knee) while he is in clear possession of the ball— perhaps as he is, say, scooping up a bad snap—the play is over. Of course, Liner said that if a player is touching the ground while the ball is loose, that's different. "If he's in the process of bringing the ball up and he's bobbling the ball while the knee is on the ground, he's not down."

Obviously there is an exception to the knee-down, play-dead rule: on points after touchdown kicks and field goal attempts, the holder is permitted to be in contact with the ground as he takes the long snap and sets the ball down for the kicker. If it's a fake kick, he simply rises up from his holding position and takes off to run or pass the ball; and that, of course, if all is well and good.

 It's a catch, and the receiver is free to get up and try for as many yards as he can muster.

 No, in fact, any time a player who has gone beyond the line of scrimmage throws the ball forward (as opposed to a lateral that is fine anywhere), he's guilty of an illegal forward pass; and it will cost his team yardage.

Sure, one can throw the ball lefty, righty, underhanded, side armed, or the traditional overhanded way. Completing the pass and picking up yards is the only thing that matters; style points are not awarded in the NFL.

Yes, by rule the catch by Addai was perfectly fine.

As described, neither the catch nor the score is valid because, unlike the situation with Addai, back in 1972 there was a rule that stipulated that, as veteran NFL official Tim Millis recalled, "As an offensive player you could not legally catch a pass that had deflected off another offensive player." No other offensive player was eligible to make the reception after it was touched by a teammate unless a defender had, in the meantime, touched the ball. That rule changed in 1978.

Now, said Millis, "If the ball deflects off any defensive player or any eligible offensive player, then any other offensive player can now catch it."

The play in question is basically a variation on what is perhaps the most famous pass play in NFL history, the Immaculate Reception made by Franco Harris. However, in that play the key difference is a defensive back, and not a fellow Steeler, *was* ruled to have touched the ball before Harris made his amazing catch.

Here's how it all played out: The Steelers hosted the Oakland Raiders two days before Christmas of 1972 in the AFC divisional playoff contest. With time running out on quarterback Terry Bradshaw and the Steelers—just twenty-two seconds remained in the game—he faced a fourth-and-ten with no time-outs left. Bradshaw was flushed out of the pocket, and still under heavy pressure, he fired a pass intended for halfback John "French" Fuqua. At about the same time, the ball neared Fuqua, and so did Oakland safety Jack Tatum; and a collision ensued, sending Fuqua sprawling, and the football headed to the artificial turf of Three Rivers Stadium.

Now, to this day nobody is positive if the ball hit off Fuqua, Tatum, or both, but the refs ruled it had hit off Tatum. Under the rules of that era, the Harris catch would be legal if the ball had either touched Tatum *or* if it made contact with both Tatum and Fuqua (no matter which man it first struck). Thus, when the football rebounded toward Harris, who was coming out of the backfield after blocking, acting as a safety valve for Bradshaw, he *was* permitted to catch the ball and did so with only five seconds left on the clock.

Controversy also remains concerning where Harris caught the ball—off the turf, which would have nullified the catch, or off his shoestrings, which is the way the refs saw it.

Therefore, after coming out of nowhere, Harris's miraculous play gave Pittsburgh a stunning victory. After a fierce scoreless first half, in a mere seventeen seconds (and one wild play) the Steelers went from being down, 7–6, to surging ahead, 12–7. Their following playoff game, the AFC Championship, did not yield such delightful results, though, as they ran into the Miami Dolphins juggernaut. The Don Shula–led squad defeated Pittsburgh en route to their historic unblemished 17–0 season and culminated with their win in Super Bowl VII.

Nevertheless, the Steelers had arrived; they were accepted, respected, a new big boy on the block. Their franchise, then forty years old, had produced only nine seasons in which Pittsburgh finished over .500; and before their incredible comeback win over Oakland, they had appeared in just one other postseason game, a 1947 loss to the Philadelphia Eagles. In 1969 they had gone 1–13; but with their emergence in 1972, they began to soar; and they would go on to become victors in four Super Bowls over a six-year span, winning the title game in January of 1975, 1976, 1979, and 1980.

Some did-you-know items: When the first Super Bowl was played (in 1967), tickets ran $6, $10, and for the best seats in the house, $12. Plus, even as game time neared, tickets were not at all difficult to come by—*The Plain Dealer* called the event "a dud at the gate." It was broadcast on both NBC and CBS, with the rights costing each network a mere $1 million. Furthermore, the winners' share was a paltry $15,000 per man versus $7,500 for the losing team. A thirty-second television ad cost $42,000. By way of contrast, by the fortieth Super Bowl the half-minute ad set companies back $2.5 million, and tickets cost $600 and $700. Winners took home $73,000, some $35,000 more than the losers.

(25) No, nothing illegal took place. Once the ball was batted in the air on the pass, it was up for grabs, fair game. At that point, even a lineman was permitted to make a catch. Plus, if you thought Locker was not allowed to swat the ball away, that's incorrect—he did the proper (and legal) thing: avoiding foolish turnovers is often a key to winning football; teams must protect the ball.

In fact, had the ball been intercepted, Washington would have been denied a drive that ended with a field goal, one that gave the Huskies a tenuous lead of 13–10 with 9:53 left in the final period of play. The Trojans rallied for a field goal of their own to knot the game, but the final score in this stunning upset was Washington 16 to 13 for USC. Erik Folk kicked the winning field goal, a twenty-two-yard boot that split the uprights perfectly with three ticks left on the clock after Locker had methodically marched his team General Sherman–like, some sixty-three yards on ten plays to set up the dramatic kick.

With the loss, USC dropped to 2–1 and 0–1 in conference play even though they entered the fray at almost a three-touchdown favorite, putting a huge crimp in their season so early in the year. They would end the year at a disappointing 5–4 mark in conference play and 9–4 overall.

Trivia item: Film legend John Wayne earned a scholarship to play football at USC but later lost it after being injured while surfing—he left the school soon after the start of his junior year. His brother Robert, however, earned a letter as a Trojan fullback in 1932.

26 No. The offensive lineman is clearly an ineligible receiver in this situation.

27 There's no need to spot the ball—it's a touchdown for Moe who slashed the plane of the end zone with ball in hand. The instant he broke the plane of the goal line, he has scored; and nothing after that can change that accomplishment, no blistering hit, no shove, nothing.

28 The rules of the day dictated a quarterback could not catch a pass—not while he had been lined up out of the T-formation that the Lions (and many teams of the day) employed. Today this play would count as a score. In fact, many teams nowadays consider throwing to their quarterback, often out of the wildcat formation.

On our play, the Lions lost yardage due to the penalty; and they lost the touchdown but went on to kick a field goal to make the score 10–3 at the half. They surrendered their lead in the early part of the final quarter, but clawed back when Layne hit Jim Doran for thirty-three-yard TD pass then held on to win a nail-biter, 17–16, marking the second consecutive season they defeated Cleveland for the championship.

29 At first blush, you call offsetting penalties on Martin and Covert, but here's what actually took place that day. Referee Jerry Markbreit, using common sense more than the rule book, decided to over-look Covert's hit, realizing he had been protecting his quarterback as a good lineman is trained to do. Markbreit wrote in his book, *Last Call*, "He didn't club him in the head, he didn't punch him, he wasn't trying to hurt him." He chose to disregard Covert's shove and punish only the Packers with a fifteen-yard walk-off and an ejection of Martin.

30 Liner said Penn State gets the ball at the point of the interception. "It's called the momentum rule. His own momentum carried him into the end zone after the reception so he would get the ball at the three-yard line."

Tim Millis, an ex-NFL field judge, said the rule applies to interceptions at the spot where the second foot of the defender comes down after the ball has been caught. "The ball has not been caught until the second foot comes down"; and on such plays, that's "normally where you put the ball."

He added that the rule "also applies to a punt or gaining possession of any loose ball like a backward pass or a fumble—a player picks it up running toward the goal line and he definitely gets his second foot down in the field of play and then he goes in the end zone and get tackled. The momentum rule would apply and he'd get the ball wherever his second foot came down. Once the momentum from the catch ends and he has gained his initiative—let's say he possesses the ball at the one, and he starts running toward the two and three and he goes back into the end zone—it's all over. It would be a safety."

Liner concurred that in college a key factor here is if the defender actually did "carry the ball in there on his own. You see that, a guy intercepts the ball and he tries to loop around and he gets caught in the end zone—that's the definition of a safety, getting tackled in your own end zone after he carried the ball in there."

31 Liner said the key to this play is if Shipley went out of bounds while going forward or backward. If he was still heading forward, "then the clock stops. If he comes to a certain position and the defender hits him and drives him out of bounds and he's still fighting, but he goes out of bounds *behind* his forward progress, then the play was over when his forward progress stopped—so his going out of bounds didn't make any difference and the clock keeps going.

"If you read the rule, the play is over and the ball is declared dead when a player's momentum is such that his forward progress is stopped. So if he's going backward, his forward progress *is* stopped."

That, he noted, ties in with "the controversial fumble rule." Say a runner's "knee isn't down but he's going backwards and the ball pops out. People say, 'Oh, it's a fumble.'" It's not, though, if the ref had ruled his progress had been stopped—the play was, in fact, dead before the ball came loose.

Did-you-know items: Shipley was not only the favorite target of McCoy, but the two young men were close friends and roommates at Texas as well. As a matter of fact, their fathers were also roommates when they attended Abilene Christian University.

Another famous roommate tandem with a quarterback-receiver connection produced one of the game's most famous college football plays ever. They were Boston College's Doug Flutie and Gerald Phelan, who was Flutie's Hail Mary target in the 1984 last-second heave that resulted in a sixty-four-yard TD over defending national champs, Miami. Final score in this wild one: BC 47 to Miami's 45.

Yet another note of interest: winning the prestigious Heisman is no guarantee of success in pro ball; and in fact, there have been some odd circumstances surrounding victories by certain players. For example, the year Paul Hornung won the Heisman Trophy, 1956, he not only beat out Jim Brown—and while Hornung was a fine runner, he was no Jim Brown—but he somehow copped the award while playing for a Notre Dame team that went 2–8 after absorbing a 40–0 clobbering by Oklahoma, a 47–14 loss to Michigan State, losing 33–7 to Navy, and being annihilated 48–8 by Iowa! Another member of the Fighting Irish, Angelo Bertelli, won the award in 1943 despite playing in just five games. It wasn't his fault as he was called into military service, but still, five games? Then there was Notre Dame quarterback John Huarte, a good college player, but one who would never enjoy the NFL fame attained by his Heisman rivals the year he won it, 1964. That year these men lost out to Huarte: Joe Namath, Gale Sayers, Dick Butkus, and Tucker Frederickson. Whatever the case may be, Notre Dame has produced more Heisman Trophy–winning players, seven (tied with Ohio State), than any other college.

Hornung would go on to have a golden career with the Green Bay Packers. He led the NFL in scoring in 1959, 1960, and 1961, aided by his ability to score on runs, catches, and placekicks. In his most prolific season, he ran for thirteen TDs, caught two passes for scores, kicked forty-one extra points, 0 goals for 176 points in twelve contests.

(32) Here's a prime example of a man who usually isn't an eligible receiver being used, quite legally, as one. On October 11, 2009, Kansas City linebacker Mike Vrabel caught a one-yard touchdown pass from Matt Cassel. He simply lined up as a receiver after reporting in to the officials that he would be doing so and would therefore be a legal receiver, got lost in the crowd, so to speak, and drifted into the end zone on a key third-and-goal play. Unfortunately for the Chiefs, they were outscored by Dallas 26 to 10 the rest of the way and wound up losing 26–20.

Vrabel's score took his offensive output to a remarkable eleven TDs on exactly eleven catches over his thirteen-year career. He even hauled in two touchdown passes in postseason play (with the Patriots).

Then there was Chicago Bears mammoth defensive lineman No. 72 William "the Refrigerator" Perry who stood six feet two and weighed in at 325 pounds, perhaps not quite as big as a Frigidaire nowadays (or as many of today's players), but big enough. He was occasionally employed on offense by Coach Mike Ditka. Effective at first, he became a not-so-secret weapon after the 1985 season. The last three times he ran with the ball—one time each in the 1986, 1987, and 1990 season—he lost two yards.

Overall Perry carried the ball eight times for five yards, but did score two touchdowns in short-yardage situations (averaging just .6 yards per rush). He added another touchdown on a four-yard toss from Jim McMahon. Two of Perry's three regular season scores, all in 1985, gave Chicago the lead, two came against the Packers, and all three came in victories for the Bears. To cap off his heroics for the 1985 heroics campaign, he scored on a run from one yard out in Super Bowl XX in the Louisiana Superdome versus the New England Patriots. His rumble into the end zone gave Chicago a 44–3 lead in a 46–10 blowout.

A note on numbers: in 1973 the NFL introduced a new jersey-numbering rule that required quarterbacks and specialists to wear a numeral between 1 and 19; runners and defensive backs had to don a uniform with a number from 20–49; linebackers had to wear 50–59; the numbers from 60–79 went to defensive linemen and the interior offensive linemen; and basically speaking, numbers from 80–89 belonged to tight ends and wide receivers. Normally then, a man wearing a number such as the one Vrabel wore would be considered an ineligible receiver—that's why he had to report in to officials prior to running a play with him lined up as a receiver. Failure to report in results in an illegal substitution call that costs a team five yards and is called even if the player never even got a whiff of the football. It is important to acknowledge, though, that a new rule now permits linebackers to wear numbers from 40-49 as well as numbers in the 50's and 90's.

The key to NFL plays involving the eligibility of players who are not normally eligible receivers is notifying the officials. If, for example, a defensive tackle was going be used as, say, a tight end, then the officials must be informed by that player that he will be employed as an eligible receiver on that upcoming play; and he must, like any true receiver, still follow rules as to where he must line up in the formation.

The reason such players must report to NFL officials is simply, explained Tim Millis, "to make the game easier to officiate and to play." He pointed out that various high school rules and certainly college rules are not like the NFL in this realm. "The pro rule has been that to be an eligible receiver you've got to be eligible by position and number. So if your number is 50 through 79, you're not eligible by number to catch a pass no matter where you line up unless you report. In fact, you're not even eligible to line up there—in the pros they go so far as to say you must have eligible receivers on the end of the line. Ineligibles report to the referee and umpire who make a waving signal with both hands in front of their chest and advise the defense, '79 has reported eligible,' and the officials point to where he is.

"Once an ineligible reports, he must stay in that eligible position until he leaves the game. Every down he has to tell the referee, 'I'm still eligible,' but they [the officials] are only required to announce it once." There are exceptions to the rule about such players staying in his given position until he departs from the field. There are eight situations including if a touchdown is scored or a safety, if there's a change of possession, if there's a time-out, if there is a replay. Any of those things allow a player who has reported to "move to another position without leaving the game. All bets are off."

Another little-known rule is a player with an eligible number must report if he is lining up in an ineligible position.

In college football players who are not usually receivers do not report to officials. Mike Liner explained, "It's numbering and where you line up." Thus, if a player enters a game wearing a number not associated with being an eligible receiver, "he's never going to be eligible."

33 On September 12, 2010, the play you're now ruling on actually happened and in a highly visible situation—it's a play you've probably seen. Detroit's Calvin Johnson secured a pass from Shaun Hill, good for an apparent game-winning catch with less than thirty seconds left in the game, and did so with both hands while leaping over the head of Chicago cornerback Zachary Bowman. Johnson lost the football, but only after shifting the ball to his right hand and also after he had plopped to the ground, landing on his left hip and thigh. It was at that point that the ball, with his hand on top of it, also hit the turf and the football bounced out of his grip. The ref stated, in what seemed like a redundant assessment, that Johnson had not completed "the catch during the process of the catch." Thus, by losing the ball; *and* due to the rule known as the Bert Emanuel rule, one that dated back to 2000, this was no catch and the Bears held on for a 19–14 victory.

The rule seems odd in that the receiver managed to enter into the end zone and plant both feet while holding the ball with two hands—that seems more likely to be deserving of a touchdown than if, say, a runner never crossed into the end zone but merely extended just an iota of the football through the plane of the goal line—which is, of course, all it takes for a run to count as a TD. Why then is one action worth six points and the other act, the Johnson play, worthless?

(34) Back in 1972 the officials did nothing about the apparent "mistake" by the operator of the clock. Given the opportunity to get off one more play, Jones lobbed a touchdown strike to Brad Davis to win the game, 17–16.

In the excellent book, *ESPN College Football Encyclopedia*, edited by Michael MacCambridge, a passage relates that Ole Miss fans "swear that time did not merely stand still that night but actually moved backward." What they perceived as an act of grand larceny led Rebel supporters to "erect a sign at the Mississippi-Louisiana state line: 'You are now entering Louisiana. Set your clocks back four seconds.'"

Trivia item: on the Ole Miss campus in Oxford, Mississippi, the speed limit is eighteen miles per hour, a speed chosen to honor Archie Manning, a great quarterback who wore that number on his jersey when he was a Rebel. He also fathered two standout quarterbacks, Eli, who also attended Mississippi, and Peyton, who chose to go to Tennessee. When these men took to the field, opponents' defenses figuratively set off air raid alarms, well aware that the Mannings were going to attack them unmercifully via the sky.

35 The rules of the day resulted in Washington being charged with an automatic safety. The goalpost also came into play later in the game after Cleveland came back to score a TD to bring the score to 8–7. Bob Waterfield's PAT attempt hit the crossbar, took a hop in the air, then fell over the bar. That, of course, made the kick good. Thus, the three points scored in the game involving odd plays pertaining to the goalpost were vital, with the Rams winning by a mere point, 15–14.

36 No interception, the ball was ruled dead once it hit the goalpost; and Baltimore had to settle for a field goal.

37 This is an interception, but Iowa went on to upset fifth-ranked Penn State, 21–10, and take them from the ranks of the undefeated.

38 Yes, due to a little-known rule, the act of having his tiptoes come down in bounds wasn't enough to make this a bona fide catch. His efforts were wiped out.

39 The rules of the day mandated a passer had to be at least five yards behind the line of scrimmage in order for the throw to be legal. If, as described in the question, Nagurski was only four yards off the line, the touchdown should have been waved off. Nevertheless, the refs that day believed Nagurski was *just* deep enough to make the play proper; and Chicago went on to win it all, 9–0.

This 1932 playoff game, which was played on a short field at Chicago Stadium (see introduction for more details), led to several rule changes. The following season officials no longer required a passer to be five or more yards deep, a pass could be thrown from anywhere behind the line. Goalposts were moved from the end line to the goal line just as they had been for the championship game; and the ball would be spotted on the hash marks for every play.

Did you know: Nagurski also wrestled professionally and is, to this day, regarded as one of the greatest collegiate football players of all time? ESPN, for instance, listed him as the seventeenth best college gridiron star in their 2007 top 25 ranking.

Another peculiar rule from the dark ages of pro football had any incomplete pass into the end zone becoming an automatic touchback with the football being given to the opponents.

(40) Naturally this counts as a fumble and should have served as a lesson to all would-be flashy show-offs. However, Smith was not the only man to celebrate and/or spike the football prematurely (think DeSean Jackson et al.)—he's not even the only Steeler to do so. In 2000 Plaxico Burress spiked a live ball in a game against Jacksonville.

ANSWERS

Perhaps the most famous instance of premature celebration took place in Super Bowl XXVII when Cowboys defensive lineman Leon Lett recovered a Frank Reich fumble at the Dallas thirty-five-yard line and began his race into the end zone. Convinced that he was about to conclude his heroic feat, Lett held the ball away from his body with a dramatic flair. Don Beebe of the Bills never gave up in his pursuit of Lett, caught him at about the one-yard line, and stripped the ball from the showboating Cowboy. The ball then went through the end zone, resulting in a touchback for the Bills. Not only didn't Buffalo surrender six points to Lett, they gained the ball as well.

(41) If you thought this call involves an ineligible receiver, no, that's not the issue here—once the pass was batted, anyone could catch it. This is simply a safety, albeit an unusual one. Give Hall a reception, Luck a completion, give Tech two points. Hall should have knocked the ball to the ground instead of catching it. Due to the safety, the first quarter ended in a baseball-like 7–2 score. From there Stanford methodically steamrolled their way to a 40–12 victory.

(42) Williams, who had already copped the 2010 John Mackey Award as the country's best tight end, was ruled to be down; and the TD was called back.

(43) As mentioned earlier, while Major League Baseball does not officially recognize the sandlot rule that a tie goes to the runner, in the world of the NFL the sort of tie described in the question does go to the team on offense. So, if you guessed the offense gets the ball in such situations in both college and pro football, you're correct.

On September 11, 2011, for example, a play like this came up when Dallas played the Jets. Miles Austin caught a Tony Romo pass, but it was also secured by New York cornerback Antonio Cromartie, apparently simultaneously. The two players grappled over the ball as they tumbled into the end zone. A Yahoo Sports website pointed out this simultaneous catch resulted in a touchdown for Dallas. An argument could have been made that Cromartie deserved credit for an interception, but that's not the way the call went. At first it seemed as if he had more control of the ball, but Austin won the wrestling match.

(44) This situation is a lot like one that takes place in baseball. If a runner misses home plate and no tag has been made, an umpire will indicate absolutely nothing. It's up to the runner to realize there's been no call and go back to touch the plate, or it's up to the fielders to see that nothing has been called by the ump and there's an immediate need to tag the runner out. In the Oregon versus Utah game the officials simply waited until Walker picked it up and then let the play proceed from there.

Coincidentally, Clay attended the same high school as another player who committed the same boneheaded play once, DeSean Jackson. In his case the play took place in a game in which his Philadelphia Eagles would have taken a five-point lead over the Dallas Cowboys during a Monday Night Football contest. Instead, when he dropped the ball prior to breaking the plane of the goal line, he cost his team a TD. Jackson, notorious for his antics, became better known on that occasion for his foolish and very premature celebratory actions.

(45) No, there is no rule that prohibits the defense from doing what the Oregon player did in this question. Had he been out of bounds when he touched the football, that would have been a different story.

(46) The play is one that is permitted to be reviewed and, in fact, the officials did scrutinize the play and allowed it to stand as a touchdown for the Ducks.

(47) False. The only reason this item is false is because a passer doesn't necessarily have to be outside the box *when he makes his throw.* He must, however, have been outside the tackle box at some point during the down.

DEANGELO
WILLIAMS

FLEET OF FOOT: THE RUNNING GAME

1 The next question involves a famous play that dates all the way back to New Year's Day of 1929. That year the contestants in the Rose Bowl were Georgia Tech and California.

The California team captain was center Roy Riegels who gained eternal notoriety on one single play, clearly a very memorable play, that day. The game was scoreless when a second-quarter fumble by Georgia Tech running back Stumpy Thomason bounced into the hands of Riegels at around the thirty-five-yard line (reports vary on this) of Tech. At first Riegels was headed for a touchdown and fame—rather than the infamy that would soon set in—as he took a few strides toward the end zone and six points.

Later Riegels analyzed what went wrong at that point, explaining that he "made a complete horseshoe turn after going four or five yards when I saw two players coming at me from the right. In pivoting to get away, I completely lost my bearings . . . I just headed the wrong way."

YOU'RE THE REF!

Recognizing Riegels's plight, his teammates soon chased after him. One of them, Benny Lom, got near to Riegels and yelled, "Stop, you're going the wrong way"; but on ran Riegels, obliviously headed toward his own end zone.

Finally, after an agonizing pursuit, Lom chased down Riegels at around the three-yard line; Riegels managed to slam on his brakes at the two-foot "line," where he was brought down by Tech tacklers. Interestingly, it was reported that Riegels had misunderstood Lom's intentions, shouting, "Get away from me. This is my touchdown."

Here's a gimme question: what would the ruling have been if Riegels had made it into the end zone and then been tackled?

Answer on page 75

(2) On the next rare, bizarre play, the refs had to make a call involving a situation that most fans have never even dreamed of.

In the Cotton Bowl held on January 2, 1954, Alabama played Rice when Dick Moegle was racing down the sideline for what would have probably been a very easy score. Suddenly, not unlike an irrational and frustrated fan ready to fire his remote at the television over his team's bad luck, Alabama fullback Tommy Lewis bolted from the Crimson Tide bench, streaked from the sidelines onto the field, and taking matters into his own arms, *tackled Moegle*! He then calmly stood up and made his way back toward the 'Bama bench.

Certainly the tackle was illegal, but what could (and did) the refs do to rectify the injustice caused by Lewis?

Answer on page 77

(3) Colorado played Missouri relatively early into their schedule back on October 6, 1990. Late in the ball game after the Buffaloes spiked the ball to kill the clock, Missouri, already ahead 31–27, stymied Colorado on two-goal-to-go situations using a stonewall defense, bringing up what should have been a fourth down.

With two seconds left in the contest, Colorado, out of time-outs and believing it to be only third down, spiked the ball once more. Perhaps they glanced over at the down marker that hadn't been changed and felt they would have time to spike the football and still get off one last play. Because nobody noticed the marker had not been updated to read fourth down, everyone was apparently mixed up; and Colorado did indeed run a play on fifth down! Quarterback Charles Johnson then scored on a short dive into the line. Was this play allowed to count?

Answer on page 78

(4) Florida State was on the road playing Boston College on October 3, 2009, and the score was tied, 21–21, in the game's final quarter. With 4:17 to go, BC had a first-and-ten from their forty-two-yard line. Running back Montel Harris took the ball, plunged up the middle, and cut sharply to his right, chased by senior safety Jamie Robinson of the Seminoles in a they're-off-to-the-races situation. At the two-yard line, Harris's right foot hit the hash mark as Robinson caught up to and made contact with him, knocking him toward the sideline. However, near the goal line pylon, Harris extended his body and the ball, held in both hands, and dove. By that time, most of his body was out of bounds, yet he was able to extend the ball so that it touched the pylon before he came down to earth. Is this a touchdown or not?

Answer on page 79

(5) This situation is nearly identical to the previous play, so it should present no big challenge for you. Penn State, already holding a commanding lead of 28–10 over Illinois, had the ball with exactly one second less than thirteen minutes to go in their game back on October 3, 2009. Junior tailback Brent Carter took a handoff, then was hit by a defender at about the two-yard line where he fell forward. His left hand, the one toting the ball, pierced the plane of the end zone. Then, a split second later when his hand hit the turf, he fumbled and the football tumbled out of bounds. Is this a safety, a touchdown for PSU, a fumble with the Fighting Illini taking over at their own twenty-yard line? Just what is the proper ruling here?

Answer on page 79

6 Let's say that it's third down and one yard to go when John Riggins of the Redskins squirms his way into a mass of bodies, managing to get only a centimeter or so beyond the yard he needed for the first down. Riggins was then met by hard-hitting Harvey Martin of the Dallas Cowboys, an impenetrable brick wall who stopped his advance altogether. Further, on this play Martin manhandled the Skins fullback, tugging him backward for two yards. Is the result of the play a net minus yard on the carry—the rugged defense robbed him of his gain—or is it a first down for Washington?

Martin, by the way, shared co-MVP honors in Super Bowl XII with teammate Randy White, marking the only time the Super Bowl had more than one MVP.

Answer on page 79

7 The next imaginary play takes place in 1972. The ball is on the one-yard line in a goal-to-go situation. Pittsburgh Steelers coach Chuck Noll has just engineered a long drive and now wants to culminate it with a satisfying go-ahead touchdown; so he calls the number of full-back Franco Harris, a rookie who was destined to reach a thousand-plus yards that season, good for the first of eight times he'd attain that plateau.

Harris, the six foot two, 230-pound future Hall of Famer, takes the handoff from Terry Bradshaw and drove ahead but is met by a troop of defenders. He bounces back, continues to churn his feet, but makes no discernable advance. His attempt to score is about to be snuffed out when running mate, the flashy John "Frenchy" Fuqua (who had, you'll recall, been involved in the Immaculate Reception and who once hit the town in a flamboyant outfit complete with platform shoes with see-through heels that contained live goldfish), plows into him from behind in an effort to give Harris momentum and to help propel him into the end zone. Sure enough, due to the impetus of the shove, Harris hit pay dirt, but is this ploy legal?

Answer on page 79

8 Twenty-first-ranked Stanford played Oklahoma in the 2009 Sun Bowl in El Paso, Texas, on the final day of the year. In the second quarter with the Sooners up, 17–14, Stanford had the ball on Oklahoma's seventeen-yard line with plenty of time (6:49) left in the first half.

Stanford relied heavily on their star running back Toby Gerhart, a bull of a runner who, after picking up some momentum, is also capable of flashing some near-equine speed, making him, at times, as difficult to grab as a watermelon seed. Weeks earlier he had finished second in the Heisman voting behind Alabama's splendid runner Mark Ingram. In fact, Gerhart's point total was only twenty-nine shy of Ingram's, making this the tightest race for the prestigious trophy ever, covering a seventy-five-year period.

Gerhart clearly deserved kudos; he scored a Stanford record twenty-six touchdowns on the regular season and he registered a career record forty-four TDs. So it was no surprise to see Gerhart taking a handoff in an effort to take the lead over Oklahoma. He pierced the middle of the Sooner defense, broke a tackle or two, and was headed for an apparent score when freshman Ronnell Lewis punched the ball from his grasp at about the two-yard line. After a mad scramble, Gerhart recovered his own fumble in the end zone for a score. It was his second touchdown on the afternoon (and twenty-eighth on the year), and his dash helped him chew up 135 yards on the day, padding his season total of 1,736 yards on the ground (giving him 1,871 overall rushing yards when his bowl performance is tossed in), best in the nation.

Your question is this: what if a teammate of his had fallen on the ball in the end zone? Would that still have been a touchdown? Note: another similar question on such a situation is also in this book, but that one deals with an NFL game.

Answer on page 83

(9) Usually when two penalties take place, one by the team on offense and the other by the defensive team, they are offsetting and the play is nullified. It doesn't matter if one of the penalties was only a five-yarder and the other called for a fifteen-yard punishment.

Say a runner hits a hole the size of Dubuque, Iowa, and picks up a ton of yards; but his team had too many men on the field during the play. Then, after his run he was bowled over when he was already out of bounds. One penalty took place during the running of the play and the other one occurred after the ball was dead. Is this still an offsetting situation, or do one (or both) of the infractions stand? Furthermore, what if one team had committed two penalties on the play to just one for the other team—is this handled in a different manner?

Answer on page 83

(10) In college ball, unlike the NFL, any time a team makes a first down, the clock is stopped. Let's say Wisconsin running back John Clay just advanced the football twelve yards on a third-and-two situation with his team desperately trying to beat the first half clock to score. The clock stops so the offense gets the opportunity to regroup, but exactly when do the officials start the clock once more?

Answer on page 85

(11) This question is similar to an earlier one concerning D. J. Williams, but with no twist of the wrist here—see if that has any bearing on your answer.

In the 2010 season opener for the Virginia Tech Hokies (No. 10) and the third-ranked Boise State Broncos, quarterback Tyrod Taylor of VT began a second-and-nine play from the Boise thirty-yard line working out of the shotgun. Already up 27–26 with 10:07 left in the game, he was trying to pad the slim lead. After looking downfield,

Taylor sprinted out of the pocket. He nearly got back to the line of scrimmage when linebacker J. C. Percy wrapped Taylor up by an ankle. Taylor lost his balance but recovered by lowering both hands to the ground; his right hand cradled the football in such a way that while that hand did in fact touch the ground, the ball never did, nor did any other part of his body.

Did Taylor's actions with his hands and/or the ball mean he was down or not?

Answer on page 85

(12) This next play may have been a run or a pass play, but it never got going at all. At any rate, here it is: The Chicago Bears had the ball against the Philadelphia Eagles in October 2007 in the final stanza of a 9–9 tie. A snap by Chicago center Olin Kreutz went though Brian Griese's legs untouched by the quarterback. The football rolled behind Griese where safety Sean Considine snatched it up. What seemed like a fumble recovery was ruled to be nothing more than a false start against the Bears. Why?

Answer on page 86

(13) Imagine the year is 1961 and New York Giants Pro Bowl fullback Alex Webster is grabbed by the face mask by Philadelphia Eagles corner back Irv Cross. How many yards would the officials have stepped off for this action back then?

Answer on page 86

(14) When Ohio State squared off against Iowa in November 2009, the Buckeyes faced a third-and-one from their own twenty-nine-yard line. Terrelle Pryor handed off to Brandon Saine who gained enough ground for a first down but coughed up the football. It bounced backward where OSU recovered the ball but not at a spot that would still give them the first down. Easy one: is it a first down or not?

Answer on page 87

(15) In a 1997 contest, Minnesota and Carolina were tied with barely over fourteen minutes to go in the game. Brad Johnson, the Vikes's quarterback at the time, was faced with a third-and-goal situation. His pass was deflected off a defender and came back to Johnson. Realizing it was illegal to pass again, he scampered and managed to score, but is this play legal? If it is, how would the play be reflected in his stats?

Answer on page 87

(16) Conjure up a picture of a running back who sets up in his own end zone, takes a handoff while still shy of the goal line, and barely gains an inch. The ref spots the ball with part of it resting directly on the goal line, with only the nose of the football out of the end zone. Is this a safety?

Answer on page 87

72

FLEET OF FOOT: THE RUNNING GAME

17 In this scenario, the year is 2009 and Baltimore's Ray Rice lugs the ball for a few yards. After the play is over and he's hopped back onto his feet, he is violently forearmed to the ground by a defender. Now, in this case we'll imagine this penalty took place on the final play of the half or of the game. What would an NFL official do here?

Answer on page 87

18 When the Cleveland Browns upset the New England Patriots in November 2010, one particular play was of interest. With 3:30 remaining in the second quarter and with the Browns up, 10–7, Cleveland's Josh Cribbs, normally a wide receiver, lined up as the team's quarterback on a first-and-ten from the New England eleven-yard line. Chansi Stuckey, a six foot tall, 196-pound receiver, crouched down behind six-foot-two, 305-pound lineman Billy Yates, trying to be as inconspicuous as possible. Yates helped by maintaining a standing position "until the last possible second." Stuckey took a handoff from Cribbs and crossed the goal line for his first rushing touchdown as a pro, but did it count?

Answer on page 88

19 During a Colts contest in 2010, Peyton Manning took off with the ball, neared the first down marker, then went into his slide to avoid being blasted by a Houston defender. Can you recall the play and the controversy it (and the rule involved) stirred up?

Answer on page 88

20 Let's say the Dolphins are in their two-minute drill as the half winds down in their contest againt the Colts. A third-down specialist runs a sweep to the far sidelines, away from the Colts bench. He gets the first down, but Miami wants to get a different runner into the game and do so without burning too much clock. In order to save time, can the back who just got the first down simply run to the opponents' side of the field, giving way to his replacement?

Answer on page 89

21 True or false: at one time a player who was running with the football could cause a play to be over by simply declaring that he was down.

Answer on page 89

ANSWERS

1 That would have been ruled a safety. As it was, shortly after Riegels's mistake, Georgia Tech blocked a Cal punt in the end zone for two points—crucial in that the Yellow Jackets would go on to win by a puny point, 8–7. From that day on, the name of Wrong-Way Riegels, who gained an iota of vindication when he later became an All-American, was carved into college football lore. He even received gag gifts from football fans such as street signs indicating wrong way and upside-down cakes.

Incidentally, by the start of the next football season, college officials put a new rule on the books stating that a player could not advance a fumble that had touched the ground. That rule lingered all the way until 1990.

Riegels's name comes up virtually any time a confused ballcarrier heads in the wrong direction. Most famously when Minnesota Viking defensive end Jim Marshall scooped up a Billy Kilmer fumble in 1964 and huffed his way into the end zone some sixty-six yards away. However, because he ran into his own end zone and threw the ball out of bounds in a celebratory gesture, he gave the 49ers a safety—a member of the 49ers then came over and patted Marshall on his back as a thank-you for the gift points.

TROY
POLLARD OF THE
UNIVERSITY OF ILLINOIS

Trivia item: at the time of the play, Kilmer was on the receiving end of a George Mira pass, but he would go on to become a quarterback himself, most famously with the Redskins.

(2) Convinced that Moegle would have scored, the refs ruled that Rice be awarded the touchdown, a ninety-five-yarder that set a record for the Cotton Bowl Classic; and Rice went on to cruise to a 28–6 win. On the day Moegle scored three touchdowns and established a Cotton Bowl record with his 265 yards rushing, a record that stood until 2008 when Missouri's Tony Temple ran for 281 yards and scored four times on twenty-four rushing attempts. Moegle's accomplishment is even more incredible given the fact that he carried the ball just eleven times, giving him a staggering average of 24.1 yards per carry.

Not only was Moegle astonished at the impromptu cameo appearance of Lewis, so was Lewis—he said he couldn't believe his own actions; he just got caught up in the moment. After the game he apologized to Moegle; and according to *Time* magazine, he "wept unashamedly in the dressing room" and "moaned: 'I don't think I'll ever get over it.'" Roy Reigels, famous for his Rose Bowl blunder, advised Lewis to laugh it off. "It's just a football game," he stated.

In 2010 a New York Jets assistant coach came close to emulating the strange play from the Rice versus Alabama game. Sal Alosi, the Jets strength and conditioning coach, tripped Miami's cornerback Nolan Carroll as the rookie was covering a punt in the third quarter, sticking out his left knee from the sidelines to do so. The next day, some strict punishment was dished out—Alosi was suspended without pay by the Jets for the rest of the season and fined $25,000.

Two days later, deeper investigation by the Jets revealed that Alosi had, according to the Associated Press, "ordered five inactive players to form a wall along the sideline for a punt return," the one that resulted in Carroll's injury. The players stood "where they were to force the gunner in the game to run around them." New York tight end Jeff Cumberland stated, "Since the beginning of the year, we've been instructed to line up behind the [white] line" by Alosi. Armed with the new damning data, the Jets upped their suspension of Alosi to one of indefinite length. In addition, the NFL later fined the Jets $100,000 because Alosi had "placed players in a prohibited area on the sideline to impede an opposing team's special teams payers and gain a competitive advantage."

3 Certainly the fifth down play should not have been permitted to occur (and the seven officials working the game were subsequently suspended by the Big 8 conference for this botched play); but as mentioned, *nobody* noticed the mistake and the touchdown stood. The commissioner of the Big 8 made this statement: "In accordance with the football playing rules, the allowance of the fifth down is not a correctable error." After defeating Missouri, Colorado went on to knock off Notre Dame in the Orange Bowl. They posted a record of 11–1–1 and were declared national champions by the Associated Press.

4 Because the ball did indeed touch the pylon before Harris hit the ground, the ball is considered to have traveled through the plane of the end zone. So this play was, after a review by the officials, called a touchdown.

5 It's a six-pointer for Carter and the Nittany Lions. Once again, once the ball slices through the end zone's plane, everything else is moot.

6 It's a first down for Riggins on this "can't miss" question. This is based on the concept of forward progress that allows the ballcarrier to be given the maximum point his momentum carried him. Thus his progress, his gain, is not lessened if he was yanked backward.

Think about it, if there was no such thing as forward progress, in theory a team loaded with men who had Herculean strength could, instead of going for clean tackles, simply wrap up runners and heave them backward any chance they could. By an absurd extension, they could push, wrestle, or virtually carry a runner into his own end zone for cheap safeties on some occasions.

7 Harris, born Franco Dok Harris in Fort Dix, New Jersey, is the son of a World War II vet and a war bride from Italy. In college he was used at

Penn State mainly as a blocking back for All-American Lydell Mitchell. Many experts were shocked, therefore, when the Steelers used their first-round '72 draft pick (number thirteen overall) to snare Harris. Mitchell wound up with the Colts and enjoyed a fine career that included three thousand-yard rushing seasons and three Pro Bowl selections, but Harris was clearly the correct choice. Mitchell would run for 6,534 yards over nine seasons while Harris, a Hall of Famer, romped for 12,120 yards during his twelve-year stint in the NFL.

As for the Harris score in this question, strictly speaking a teammate cannot aid a ballcarrier as described in this play. In practice, though, plays like the one described in this question involving Harris do occur and are sometimes overlooked by refs.

What follows is an account of perhaps the most famous case of one teammate giving a hand/shove to help him score:

On October 5, 2005, Notre Dame (number nine in the country) played host to the USC Trojans, who were enjoying a twenty-seven-game winning streak as they sat atop the national polls. Per tradition, the night before the game, each Irish helmet had a fresh coat of paint applied to it with, get this, paint containing a small amount of gold dust.

The Irish also came out wearing their special green jerseys, pumped up and eager to renew their intense rivalry. When Notre Dame played USC in 1977, Dan Devine (a fitting name for a coach on this Catholic campus) broke out the green jerseys to spur his players on—it worked; the Irish won by thirty points and went on to capture one of their eleven national titles. On another occasion, Coach Gerry Faust ordered his troops to don the uniform at halftime in yet another win over the Trojans.

As the 2005 game wound down, the Irish held a tenuous 31–28 lead, but USC had the ball with seven seconds on the scoreboard and about a yard to go for a game-winning touchdown. At that point, Trojans coach Pete Carroll signaled to his quarterback, Matt Leinart, to spike the ball, ostensibly to set up a field goal that would knot the game and send it into overtime. That, however, was all part of an elaborate deke; the real call was a quarterback sneak. Leinart's initial surge into the line was stymied, and it appeared as if the Irish had won it. Then came *the* play. Running back Reggie Bush pushed Leinart forward, and he scored a highly controversial touchdown, one which Notre Dame fans might call a Bush League Play.

The USC winning streak was intact thanks to what actually came to be known as the Bush Push, and the defending national champs took their 6–0 record and upped it to a perfect 12–0 slate by regular season's end, only to drop their first game in an eon in the 2006 Rose Bowl, losing to the Vince Young–led Texas Longhorns. Going into this title game, USC was riding the nation's longest active win streak (thirty-four in a row); and Texas, with nineteen straight wins, had the second longest streak going. Fans of the legendary Keith Jackson, whose voice and famous lines became synonymous with NCAA football, also recall that this game marked his final college football broadcast.

Former college line judge Mike Liner went into more depth on plays such as the Bush Push, commenting, "The college rule is very clear: a teammate cannot aid the runner—in other words come in from behind and push him to gain an extra yard or to push him into the end zone; but when is the last time you saw that called? You never see it called. We just don't call it—it's a subjective call, one that is *really* subjective to your opinion of what happened. And it so rarely happens you don't see it enough for anybody to [get a good fix on it]. So my opinion of what aiding a runner is on a play that I see once every three or four years—I'm just not going to do that. Quite frankly, I've seen more guys get criticized for making that call than I've ever seen for anybody making it and [someone says], 'Correct call.'"

This rule pertaining to boosting a runner, trying to propel him across the goal line, is one that Ed Dohanos also finds as peculiar. "You get down to the goal line, there's a pile, two offensive backs will come in there and push the quarterback or halfback into the end zone—or even a tackle can come around and push in. That's aiding and abetting—it's a five-yard penalty, but it's never called," he chuckled. "It just doesn't happen. I've only seen it called one time—in high school they pushed the ballcarrier into the end zone."

Liner went on, "I don't know of any major conference official that's going to be around for very long that's going to make that call.

ANSWERS

There's just certain calls you just don't make. It's kind of like [ignoring] the sock stuff or mouthpieces or shirt tails or too many towels on a player. We look at that stuff before the game, but when the game starts that stuff is just background noise—we're so intent on trying to get the big things right, we don't worry about [little stuff]. If you have an official running around during a game worried about somebody having on too many towels, or the towel is not in the right spot, or it's too long, or socks aren't all the same length, or he hasn't got his mouthpiece in, then that guy isn't paying attention to what he's supposed to be. So I'm always suspect of those types of officials."

One such nickel-dime rule states only one lineman and one back may have a towel in their possession for the team on offense. "And they have to be no more than 12 inches long and four inches wide and they can't be on the back, they have to be on the hip or in the front of the player."

8   No, the fumble recovery would not count as a touchdown. A fumble that goes forward and into the end zone cannot be retrieved for a TD by any offensive player other than the man who originally lost the ball.

9   This is not a case of offsetting penalties because, as Liner pointed out, one was a live ball infraction and the other, treated differently, was in a dead ball situation. Both penalties would be enforced.

He added an interesting twist involving two penalties occurring on a play, this time with both occurring in live ball situations. "This happened to me one time: the offensive team was running a play—it was a long run and it went way downfield—but beyond the line of scrimmage the offensive team had a clip, but the [running back] ran on and on and on then gets tackled by the face mask. Both of those are live ball fouls so they offset and you replay the down, but what happened was had 'B' not fouled, 'A' [the ballcarrier and his team] would have had a first down even after the penalty. You would have gone back to the spot of the foul—because the run went beyond the foul—penalize 15 yards and re-play the down; but that still would have given 'A' a first down. By 'B' fouling, they went back to the line of scrimmage and re-played the down—his committing a foul actually helped the defense." In other words, after the first infraction had been committed, the offense still would have had a first down, but after the second foul, the first down was lost. "It was one of those unusual deals where a foul benefited the offenders."

As for the other question posed here: even if one team was guilty of two penalties on a play versus their opponents' one penalty, normally it's an offsetting situation. Say the defense was offside and the offense was guilty of illegal motion, but one team was also called for unsportsmanlike conduct. The first two penalties offset one another but the other call in this case would stand. Liner explained, "You can't let [a team] have a free shot."

(10) Liner said, "Typically, it's when the down box is set. Hopefully [the official] does it with the same tempo at the beginning of the game that he does at the end of the game." So the ref watches the chains moving but "whenever the down box is set that's when he starts the 25-second clock."

(11) No, Taylor was not down, but he would have been if the football (or wrist, knee, etc.) had made contact with the ground. He continued his run, picking up eleven yards. The Hokies would go on to kick a field goal at the 7:38 mark, but Kellen Moore engineered a masterful late drive to pull out the 33–30 victory for the Broncos.

In a more famous play involving the rule about being down or not, Auburn's freshman runner Michael Dyer came up with a big run of thirty-seven yards versus Oregon in the January 2011 BCS championship game. In the final minutes of that thriller, albeit an unexpectedly low-scoring one, Dyer was hit after a gain of about six yards, but he rolled over Oregon's Eddie Pleasant without his knee touching the ground (as was verified by an official's review). It appeared to most that Dyer was down, and nearly everyone acted as if the play was over. Hearing no whistle, though, Dyer bounced back up, hesitated a moment, then took off. His run, along with his subsequent sixteen-yard jaunt down to the one-yard line, set up the nineteen-yard game-winning Wes Byrum field goal that took place as time ran out on the clock. That gave Auburn an immaculate 14–0 record and its first national title since 1957. It also gave the Southeastern Conference a 7–0 record in BCS championship games, meaning that conference had captured more national titles than all the other conferences put together.

(12) A very obscure NFL rule states that if a snap goes through a quarterback's legs untouched when he is under center, once an opponent picks the ball up behind the QB, the play is over and a false start call is in order. Instead of losing the ball and perhaps the game, Chicago only lost five yards. Had Griese been working out of the shotgun and the ball had been snapped over his head, the play would, of course, have continued.

Chicago went on to kick a field goal giving them a 19–16 lead that held up, frustrating Philadelphia.

(13) Under the rules of that era, it was permitted to grab the face mask of the ballcarrier (but no other player). In January of the following year, a rule was drawn up to prohibit the grabbing of a face mask of an opposing player, either in blocking or tackling, and the cost of such actions was fifteen yards.

ANSWERS

(14) No first down was awarded as the ball was spotted where the football was retrieved. Still, the Buckeyes went on to win in overtime to earn a berth in the Rose Bowl. There, in Pasadena, they prevailed over Oregon, 26–17.

(15) The Johnson run counted. He was credited with a pass completion to himself, so the official summary of the score states, "Brad Johnson 3 yard pass from Brad Johnson," and the Vikings went on to win by a 21–14 score.

(16) Yes, this is a safety. As NFL rules state, it's a safety "when the ball is dead on or behind a team's own goal line if the impetus came from a player on that team."

Tim Millis, who officiated in two Super Bowls, clarified this play, "To get it out [of the end zone], the entire ball has got to get out. Any part of the ball has got to touch the plane of the goal line going in to be a touchdown. Coming out, until you get it completely out, it's still in the end zone."

(17) Prior to 2010, a dead ball foul on the final play of a half or game led to no penalty being enforced, although the league could fine a player for, say, illegal rough actions. Now, according to an AP report, the foul "will cause a 15-yard penalty on the second half or overtime kickoff."

In addition to the ruling on dead ball penalties (as described in this question), a new rule went into force in 2015 stating that if an unsportsmanlike penalty is called at the end of a half, it will carry over to either the second half or into overtime play.

(18) Yes, the Stuckey score counted—there was nothing wrong with the way the Browns lined up or with how they executed the play. Ed Dohanos, who was working on the chain crew that day, recalled that the baffled defense "had no idea where the ball was. That was great, probably one of the best [trick plays I've seen.]"

(19) The NFL rule book indicated a ballcarrier is permitted to go into a feet-first slide to avoid being hit. It further states that the ball is dead on such plays when the player hits the ground. Now, while Manning began this slide before making the first down, the spot where he hit the turf was beyond the first down marker.

The problem and controversy here is that while the league is protecting players such as Manning (which is all well and good), they are also rewarding them with extra yardage gained while they are airborne and immune from contact, rendering the defense impotent. It almost makes a head coach wish his quarterbacks had long jumping training. Critics opined that the rule should dictate the ball be spotted at the point where a slide begins, not at a distant landing point.

20 Dohanos firmly stated, "You can't do that. He [the player departing the game] has to come across the field." In other words, he must leave by going to his side of the field and only his side.

21 If you guessed true on this one because the question just seems so outrageous it wouldn't even be in this book unless it were true, you're right! Liner referred to a copy of the 1952 NCAA rule book regarding one factor that then caused a ball to be considered dead. The rule seems as archaic as it is crazy. It specified that the ball was no longer alive if, explained Liner, "the ballcarrier cried, 'Down!' So if he's down, or almost down, or being hit, and he hollers out, 'Down! Down! Down!' then the ball's dead. They had that in the old days to avoid fumbles. You can imagine the can of worms *that* opened up because then the guy gets hit and he's going down and he fumbles the ball and he starts crying, 'Down, down, down.' Now, which came first? Did the ball come loose or did he cry, 'Down'? So they took that out of the rule book."

RYAN LONG OF
SYRACUSE UNIVERSITY

BOOTING THE BALL: THE KICKING GAME

1 Say a Georgia Tech punter, with his team pinned deep into its own territory, takes a low snap; and by the time he can get the ball off, it's partially blocked. The ball rebounds behind him and slightly to his right. He scrambles and retrieves the ball. He can certainly try to run or pass for the first down, but is he permitted to punt the ball once more?

Answer on page 107

2 Trick question that involves knowledge of the history of the rules of the NFL. Let's say the year is 1966 and Dallas Cowboys punt returner Bob Hayes, once billed as the world's fastest human, is back to take a boot off the foot of Chicago Bears punter Bobby Joe Green. Hayes decides to raise his arm, signaling for a fair catch. The defense pulls up a bit, relaxing because they know there is no chance for a return. At that point, Hayes lowers his arm but lays a wicked block on one of the coverage men. If you were the ref, would you throw your flag on the play?

Answer on page 107

3 November 7, 2009. The scene is Beaver Stadium, home to the number eleven-ranked Penn State Nittany Lions. It is a setting in which occasional lion roars blare over the PA system as fans cheer on their team that is always dressed in a simple yet dignified style, unadorned by players' names on the jerseys. The team colors, blue and white, have been used since 1890.

The visitors that day were the Ohio State Buckeyes, then ranked sixteenth in the nation. As the first half was nearing its completion, Jeremy Boone punted the ball to the Buckeyes. OSU's Jaamal Berry backpedaled away from the punt in an effort not to touch the ball, but he accidentally made contact with the hopping football. At that point, still backpedaling, Berry was able to pounce on the ball in the end zone, ending the play. Was this ruled a safety or a touchback?

Answer on page 107

4 Another imaginary situation: the UCLA Bruins have just scored a touchdown against Arizona to bring the game to within three points. They now must kick off to Arizona; but with only seconds left on the clock, they elect to try an onside kick. The kicker decides to employ the method in that he sort of pokes at the ball with his foot near the top of the football that is perched on a tee. The ball then takes a quick skip off the turf and bounds high in the air, up for grabs, almost like a Hail Mary play. Now, rather than try to catch the ball among thick traffic, a player on the receiving end bats it forward and out of bounds. Is this tactic legal? Does the receiving team take over where the ball left the playing field? Just how would this work out?

Answer on page 107

(5) Tulane Stadium in New Orleans is the scene for the next question. On November 8, 1970, the Saints trailed the Detroit Lions, 17–16, with only scant seconds left. Tom Dempsey of the Saints had kicked three field goals, employing the old traditional straight-ahead kicking style since replaced by the soccer-style method; but it appeared his kicks would not be enough. New Orleans certainly seemed headed to a pathetic 1–6–1 record on the year.

The Lions had just scored an eighteen-yard field goal to give them their one-point lead with just eighteen seconds left in the contest. Billy Kilmer tossed a seventeen-yard pass to receiver Al Dodd who then scampered out of bounds at the New Orleans thirty-seven-yard-line to stop the clock.

Dempsey, born with a right club foot with no toes (as well as a fingerless right hand), used a special shoe on that (half of a) foot for his kicking chores, and he was effective. However, he was now faced with the daunting task of kicking a football sixty-three yards with just two seconds left on the clock; and he would be, as Michael Lewis wrote, "kicking from a dirt surface churned up like a World War I battlefield." The Lions were incredulous—the Saints, they wondered, weren't serious, were they?

YOU'RE THE REF!

In fact, *could* they be serious? According to NFL rules, were they permitted to kick a field goal on second down?

Answer on page 108

(6) Let's say a punt return specialist is stationed right around midfield with his team down by a point. The punt comes directly to him; and with only two seconds on the clock, he has two thoughts: (1) with excellent coverage barreling down on him, he has virtually nowhere to go. Try for a miraculous return? If he fails to score, the clock runs out and a defeat is registered. (2) Call for a fair catch and put his team's fate in the hands of his quarterback? Could a Hail Mary pass pull the game out? (3) Employ a special rule sometimes called the free kick, the fair-catch kick, or the free-kick field goal. As a ref, you must know all the rules, so what exactly is entailed here on the rare free kick—can it be used here?

Answer on page 109

(7) Imagine the Buffalo Bills have just scored a touchdown to give them an overwhelming twenty-point lead. They line up to convert the extra point when their quarterback, set deep in the backfield, drops the ball to the turf. Despite the shape of a football, it takes a clean hop; and he then kicks it through the uprights. Is this a proper kick, good for the extra point?

Answer on page 110

8 Oklahoma and Texas met in the neutral site of the Cotton Bowl in Dallas, Texas, for the 2009 edition of the long-standing Red River Shootout, a great rivalry featuring these teams vying for the Golden Hat trophy.

Both teams are rich in tradition. For example, Oklahoma is famed for, among other things, their cannon that fires at certain points in the team's home contests such as after an OU score. This tradition is a tie-in to the Boomers, that is, the Oklahoma settlers who set out to claim land upon hearing a cannon shot that signaled the official start of the Oklahoma Territory Land Run of 1889, and to the Sooners, those who didn't bother to wait for the signal and set out early to stake their land claims. Then there's Oklahoma's omnipresent Conestoga wagon that has been known to circle the field during games, make a short trip "around the goalpost after scores," and which, in a game against Washington in the 1985 Orange Bowl, Oklahoma "drew a 15-yard unsportsmanlike conduct penalty when the Schooner rolled onto the field to celebrate" a score (which was called back due to a penalty on that play).

This is also the team that once ran up a string of forty-eight consecutive games without a loss, doing so from 1953–1957 under legendary coach Bud Wilkinson, who also captured three national titles.

The game promised to be a slugfest—after all, the 2009 collegiate season featured the first time ever that three Heisman Trophy finalists from the previous year returned to their campuses the following year; and two of them (Tim Tebow, of Florida, was the other one) were starting today's game, Colt McCoy for the Longhorns and Sam Bradford, recovered from an injury, for the Sooners. A true shootout seemed imminent with points expected to pile up on the scoreboard like a pinball machine in the hands of a wizard.

In the second quarter of the contest, Oklahoma kicked to Jordan Shipley, who was tackled cleanly; but face masking was called on a player from the kicking team, Joseph Ibiloye, who was not in the vicinity of Shipley but was engaged with a Texas blocker, tugging on his mask to help shed that blocker. Is it possible for someone not making a tackle to be guilty of face masking, or was this call overturned?

Answer on page 111

9 In the same Oklahoma versus Texas contest of October 17, 2009, mentioned above, the Sooners received a punt, fielded by Dominique Franks, on about the twenty-nine-yard line where he was hit immediately and quite sharply by John Chiles, causing Franks to fumble. The ball went backward to about the eighteen-yard line, shot out of Franks's hands, and was scooped up by Malcolm Williams of Texas who attempted to take it into the end zone. He was thwarted when Brandon Crow of the Sooners, who had been in hot pursuit, managed to jar the ball loose from Williams's arms at around the two-yard line. The ball then flew into and out of the end zone—at the side, not the rear of the end zone. Because Williams never crossed the goal line with the ball, it can't be a touchdown; but just what is it—a safety, a touchback? Who gets possession of the football? What's your call?

Answer on page 113

(10) Say the old St. Louis Cardinals are playing the Chicago Bears; and the Cardinals have just punted to the Bears return man Gale Sayers, "the Kansas Comet." Sayers possessed the uncanny ability to plant a foot, cut, and change directions rapidly, making him a human slinky— here for a moment, then gone the next. Once in the open field, his long strides were as rapid and rhythmic as a strobe light.

In this case, however, the football doesn't travel all the way to the future Hall of Famer, and the entire receiving team backs off the ball, content to let it roll to a stop. Suddenly, the ball happens to take a peculiar hop and hits off Sayer's foot, even as he was retreating from the football. It then ricochets directly toward the hands of a defender who deftly fields the ball on a bounce like a Gold Glove shortstop gobbling up a routine grounder and rambles into the end zone. Is he permitted to do this, or is the ball dead?

Answer on page 113

(11) For the sake of this question, we'll have Ted Ginn, Jr., in a moment of folly, fielding a punt at the one-yard line. His backpedaling action as he is catching the football takes him into the end zone a moment after he secured the ball. Is he permitted to run it out?

Answer on page 113

(12) Now imagine a punt is blocked by a college player who then smothers the ball while on the ground. Then he laterals it to a nearby teammate who then glides into the end zone with the quickness of a flat stone skimming across the smooth surface of a pond. Is the ball dead, or is this a touchdown?

Answer on page 114

(13) Another simple one: What if the punt had been blocked and had caromed all the way into the end zone where a defender hopped on it? Is this a safety, touchback, or touchdown?

Answer on page 114

(14) Here are some facts concerning Cowboys Stadium that will lead up to the next question. The facility is about the size of fifty-five football fields, and is capable of holding an NFL-high one hundred thousand spectators. The video board that hangs 90 feet above the field extends 160 feet, looming over the field between the twenty-yard lines.

   If a punter booted the ball so high it struck the video board, what ruling would you make?

Answer on page 114

BOOTING THE BALL: THE KICKING GAME

(15) Few people in the arena knew about an obscure NFL rule involving a play that took place in a Chicago versus St. Louis contest in 2008. The Rams tried a fake punt, utilizing Eric Bassey as a receiver, lining him up as the end man on the line of scrimmage. He was tackled as the football was in midair. Why wasn't this called pass interference?

Answer on page 114

(16) If a punt bounces on, say, the five-yard line, then crosses the plane of the goal line, under what circumstances is it permissible for a college player from the coverage team to swat the ball back out of the end zone territory, downing the football in poor field position for the receiving team and avoiding a touchback?

Answer on page 115

(17) If you were working an NFL game, what would you rule if an onside kick advanced only eight yards, was untouched by both teams, then rolled out of bounds?

Answer on page 115

(18) The year is 1965 and a new rule involving fair catches is the key to this play. Let's say a player signaled for a routine fair catch. Then, seeing the ball take a hop not far from where he was positioned, he figures that if he runs up on the ball and fields it on the fly, he is bound to turn in a solid return. Is he permitted to do this? Why or why not?

Answer on page 116

19 When Ohio State defeated Oregon in the Rose Bowl on New Year's Day in 2010, they had taken a 19–17 lead deep into the third period, but the Ducks were driving on them, reaching the eighteen-yard line. Oregon runner LeGarrette Blount fumbled a handoff, then kicked it (apparently accidentally) into the end zone. Ohio State got the ball on the touchback, relieved at having thwarted the attack. Oregon would not score any more points while the Buckeyes tacked on seven more to win it, 26–17.

Now, what would the refs have called if Blount had been ruled to have purposely kicked the ball?

Answer on page 116

20 A college player is charging the punter; and after just failing to block the ball, his impetus carries him into the kicker, knocking him down. The call here is clearly roughing the kicker, but what if the player merely brushes the punter after making an obvious attempt to avoid contact? Would a ref still be required to toss his penalty marker?

Answer on page 117

21 What about an NCAA situation in which a player rushing a punter gets blocked into his target—he didn't willfully make contact, but he did plow him over—what's your call?

Answer on page 118

(22) Place kickers, like punters, are also protected by rules from contact—you can't just barge into kickers as they are in the act of doing their job—but what about the holder on kicks in the college game?

Answer on page 118

(23) What about this NCAA scenario: a player blocks a kick, be it a punt or field goal, then his momentum carries him into the kicker or the holder. Is this permitted?

Answer on page 119

(24) During a college game, a punt hits the ground and begins to roll. It then touches a man from the kicking team even though he tried to avoid contact. Is the ball dead as if that defender had intentionally downed the ball, or is it still alive?

Answer on page 119

(25) At the college level, what happens if a team tries an onside kick and the ball travels only eight yards, and the kicking team touches the ball at that spot and gains possession of it—how is this situation dealt with?

Answer on page 120

(26) Is there a limit to the number of laterals a team can execute?

Answer on page 121

(27) In NFL play, can a member of the defensive team position himself near the goalpost on a field goal attempt, then leap up to block a low-flying kick?

Answer on page 122

(28) Way back in 1939, the Washington Redskins battled the New York Giants in what was then called the Eastern Professional Championship game. An extra $1,000 per man was at stake as place kicker Beau Russell tried a potential game-winning field goal during "the dying seconds" of the contest.

An account of the day reported that the football "went sailing over one of the uprights in the dreary gloom of the Polo Grounds." Referee Bill Halloran perceived the ball to have traveled in such a path that if there had been, say, a line extending directly skyward from the upright, that line would have dissected the ball. What was his call that day?

Answer on page 122

(29) Number one Oregon met California in November 2010 and nearly got upset. On the first play of the fourth quarter, Cal set up for a twenty-four-yard field goal—if good, it would have put the Golden Bears up by a 16–15 count. However, left-footed place kicker Giorgio Tavecchio mistimed the count and took a stutter step just a fraction of a second before the snap. That motion, the moving prior to the snap, cost the Bears five yards and perhaps the game because on the next kick, now a twenty-

nine-yard attempt, Tavecchio, who had never missed from that distance over his three-year career, did just that, pulling it far to the right.

Your question: would Tavecchio have been permitted to take his stutter step, reset himself for a second or so, then kick the ball without incurring a penalty?

Answer on page 123

(30) Here's a crazy field goal play from 2007: Cleveland was being hosted by Baltimore and the Browns were looking at the short end of a 30–27 score with only three seconds left in the game. Phil Dawson was called upon to try a fifty-one-yard field goal. The football hit off the upright, struck off the curved stanchion of the goalpost, that is to say the extension that runs from the crossbar down to the ground, caromed once again, and incredibly flew back onto the playing field. Does the kick count or not?

Answer on page 123

(31) Heinz Field was the setting for the Steelers versus the Chargers AFC Divisional Playoff game on January 11, 2009. In the third quarter Pittsburgh, leading 21–10, was forced to punt. Mitch Berger's kick wobbled then hit off the helmet of a San Diego blocker, Eric Weddle. The football then took a bounce off the turf and into the hands of Pittsburgh's William Gay, who never broke stride and easily scored from twenty-three yards out. How should you unravel this play?

Answer on page 123

(32) During the 2010 matchup between Ole Miss and Tennessee, a punt by Mississippi's Tyler Campbell glanced off Janzen Jackson's hand, then rolled away from him, not too far from the famed checkerboard end zone. Brandon Bolden, of Mississippi, scrambled for the ball that appeared to squirt off his fingertips. About a second later, he skidded out of bounds, then grabbed for the football with about half of his body still out of bounds. Assuming he then gained full control of the ball, what would the refs rule here?

Answer on page 124

(33) On October 9, 2010, Texas Tech, tied with Baylor, tried to catch their foe off guard with an onside kick. Tech would have been better off forgetting the ploy and simply placed a "Kick Me" sign on their backs—the trick backfired.

The dribbler of a kick traveled just eight yards; and four players, three from the Red Raiders who seemed oblivious of the rules involved here, basically became spectators for a few seconds, watching the ball sit on the thirty-eight-yard line, unmoving. Then the Baylor player, Terrance Ganaway, alertly picked up the ball and took off for a touchdown and a 13–7 lead in the game. Fortunately for Texas Tech fans, they scratched their way back to win it, 45–38.

If Ganaway had not grabbed the football, generally speaking how long would a ref have waited before blowing the play dead once the ball came to a stop?

Answer on page 124

34 During an NFL game, a field goal is attempted on third down. It's blocked, and the kicking team gets the ball back behind the line of scrimmage. Can they kick again on fourth down? What if they got the ball back but it had traveled beyond the line of scrimmage?

Answer on page 124

35 When Dallas and Philadelphia met on Thanksgiving Day in 2014, there was no brotherly love nor giving of any thanks whatsoever, especially on one particular play. The Eagles punted the ball towards return artist Dwayne Harris. Nolan Carroll streaked down the field, prepared to make a tackle or down the ball, but as he approached the five-yard line and looked skyward to locate the ball, he was leveled by Harris on a vicious block in which Harris threw a forearm with the force of a heavyweight prize fighter's roundhouse. Harris, not at all near to where the football landed, clearly had no intention of fielding the ball, which bounded into the end zone after first hitting the ground near the goal line.

Your call: is this legal because Harris was preventing Carroll from possibly downing it on, say, the one-yard line, or was the obvious cheap shot enough to make you throw your flag? If there is a penalty here, how many yards did it cost Harris? Another consideration: would you eject him from the game or not?

Answer on page 124

JEREMY BOONE
AND
COLLIN WAGNER

ANSWERS

1   As long as the ball never crossed the neutral zone, the punter may again boot the ball.

2   As indicated, this is a trick question; and the truth is that if you had been a ref that season, you would ignore the cheap block thrown by the return man. In fact, you would have ignored it any season prior to 1967. It wasn't until February of that year that the rule makers decided to, as Pat Livingston of the *Pittsburgh Press* reported, "eliminate 'cheap shots' by punt returners who call for a fair catch and block an opponent. The rule change, introduced by Dan Rooney, will make it a personal foul when a punt return man, after calling for a fair catch, initiates contact with an opponent."

3   The loose ball was certainly live, and had PSU taken possession, they would have scored six points. But Berry had the right to pursue the ball, and because the Buckeyes recovered the ball, it was treated as a touchback.

4   Mike Liner stated, "He can't bat the ball forward. If you bat it forward, the penalty is 15 yards from that spot and they'd get the ball there."

5 This, of course, was an easy one. The down doesn't matter. A team may kick the ball on any down. The Saints were serious even though Detroit's star lineman Alex Karras later confessed that he felt the kick attempt was so absurd, bordering on sheer futility, that he didn't even rush the kicker on the play.

So the Dempsey kick on the final play of the game was not only legal, it was also good, sending his Saints to a stunning 19–17 win and sending 66,000-plus fans home in utter amazement. Dempsey later stated, "I don't think I could kick one that long in practice. There was no wind, but I knew I could kick it long enough. I just hoped I could kick it straight enough."

Dempsey said the kick came from the "closed-in area of Tulane Stadium," a horseshoe-shaped facility, where the wind "sometimes would swirl and push balls wide." He added that he got a perfect snap from Jackie Burkett and a perfect hold from Joe Scarpati and that the ball "seemed like it took forever to get there. I just kept watching it, wondering if it had enough distance. Finally, the referees raised their hands that it was good."

Some twenty-eight years later Denver's Jason Elam became the only man to match Dempsey for distance, with his sixty-three-yarder coming against Jacksonville on October 25, 1998. His historic kick took place at the end of the first half in old Mile High Stadium in Denver and helped his Broncos boost their record to 7–0, marking the first time the team had recorded an untarnished record that deep into a season. Elam was asked if he had considered backing up a yard in order to break Dempsey's record. "Well," he mused, "that gets kind of scary when you do that." Still, he said that he "really did feel I could get the ball there, but those goalposts looked really skinny from where I was standing. I'm perfectly happy with being in his company."

Incidentally, the longest recognized field goal in organized football was a whopping sixty-nine-yards long in NAIA play. The kicker was Ove Johansson of Abilene Christian; and he accomplished his feat on October 16, 1976, against East Texas State at Abilene's Shotwell Stadium (where the football did indeed shoot well *and far* off his foot) kicking off a two-inch tee.

6 Under football rules, a team that makes a proper fair catch is then permitted to try a field goal *from the spot of the catch*. The team then lines up on that field location, the opposing team must line up ten or more yards downfield; and according to Wikipedia, "The kicker then may either place kick the ball from a teammate's hold [a kickoff tee may be used in high school] or drop kick the ball." Beyond those stipulations, all the other rules for field goals are in effect (for instance, if the kick falls short, a return man for the other team can run it back); and the clock resumes its countdown once the ball is booted. College rules do not include this gimmicky play.

The most famous case of a free kick is the Dempsey field goal from the previous question. Meanwhile, Wikipedia states that through the end of the 2009 NFL season, the last time a free kick was executed for three points came in 1976 when Ray Wersching of the San Diego Chargers kicked a forty-five-yarder at the end of the first half in a game against the Buffalo Bills. After Wersching, several attempts have been made in regular season, preseason, and postseason play including a desperation try, a sixty-nine-yarder, by Mason Crosby of the Packers when they took on the Lions on December 28, 2008.

(7) The drop kick described is perfectly legal. When the shape of the football was rounder, prior to 1934, it would bounce truer than today's ball. Thus, such kick attempts—back when the game of football was more of a ground and kicking game than a passing parade, placing an emphasis on the "foot" in football—were not viewed as sideshow oddities.

The last man to attempt *and make* a once-normal, now-unorthodox drop kick was Doug Flutie on January 1, 2006, in the final game of his career. The forty-three-year-old quarterback, sporting number 2 on his Patriots jersey, had never before, nor would he ever again, kick a PAT (although he had fooled around on the side with the art of drop kicking); but this one, in a meaningless contest between New England and the victorious Miami Dolphins, was a classic.

ANSWERS

ESPN's website reported that with 6:10 left in the game, right after Tim Dwight had scored on a nine-yard TD, Flutie trotted onto the field along with the kicking unit, forcing a puzzled Dolphins coach, Nick Saban, to call a time-out. "I couldn't figure out what was going on. They had a quarterback in, four tight ends and a receiver and there was no kicker." Flutie took a snap out of a deep shotgun formation, standing on the twelve-yard line, dropped the football, and kicked it a split second after it skipped off the turf. Saban later commented that he was happy to see someone still knew how to drop kick, "but, you know Flutie showed his age on that one."

Flutie's was the first successful drop kick in NFL play since 1941 NFL, and Flutie's coach Bill Belichick said it might take another sixty years before anyone sees this play again.

The '41 kick took place in the NFL championship game on December 21 and came off the foot of Ray "Scooter" McLean of the Bears in a 37–9 pounding of the Giants.

According to the NFL rule book's simple definition, a drop kick is "a kick by a kicker who drops the ball and kicks it as, or immediately after, it touches the ground."

8 Although one almost always sees a tackler or a would-be tackler commit face masking, any player can be caught with his hand in the face mask "till," so to speak. Imagine if a player was permitted to yank on another's mask—anarchy and multiple trips to hospitals would result. Fifteen yards were added on to the Shipley run back.

This Texas-Oklahoma clash never lived up to its hype as far as pyrotechnics go, an offensive splurge never materialized as the offenses were more popgunlike rather than explosive. The final score was 16–13, with third-ranked Texas squeaking by the number-twenty-rated Sooners, a squad hamstringed when Bradford once more was injured early on—this time sidelined by a hard Aaron Williams sack. At times the swarming Oklahoma defense antici-pated plays so well it was as if they were comprised of eleven mind readers. At the half they held the Longhorns to just three points and 2.6 yards per play on offense. However, by game's end, the 104th game in the rivalry, Oklahoma dropped to 3–3 on the year while Texas soared to 6–0.

An aside: in another game, Texas versus Texas A & M on Thanks-giving Day 2009, a somewhat similar face-masking play took place in the fourth quarter of a wild and wooly one (eventually nailed down by Texas, 49–39, to preserve their unblemished record of 12–0). Texas had averaged giving up 13.3 points per game going into the contest; but with 8:21 left on the clock, the Longhorns had already surren-dered thirty-two points to the Aggies.

Texas A & M, scrambling to draw closer to Texas, called for a pass play from the Texas thirty-six-yard line. Ryan Swope took a pass from Jerrod Johnson and scampered just inside the ten-yard line. After receiving the ball, Swope had stiff-armed a would-be tackler—certainly a legal move—but, in the process, placed his hand inside his face mask and yanked on it. The catch counts, but Swope was penalized.

A few did-you-know items: the rivalry between these two schools has been intense since seemingly forever. In 1908 a brawl broke out that was so violent a University of Texas fan was stabbed in his head three times. Team mascots have been kidnapped over the years—making off with a dog, the A & M mascot, is one thing; but kidnapping a massive longhorn is a daunting task.

9 The announcers initially called the play a touchdown, but that was inaccurate. Actually the refs ruled that Texas owned the ball; and they took over where the fumble occurred, saying that the defense could not "advance the muff."

10 The ball is certainly live and it is a score. They were well aware of the rule that states that if the football touched them on such a play, it was as is if they possessed it (and in this case, then lost it). Ergo, after the football hopped off Sayers, the ball is treated exactly as if he had fumbled it.

11 Of course a return man can run (or attempt to run) a ball out of the end zone—that's always a runner's option even if it may be a risky one.

(12) This question illustrates one of the fundamental differences between NFL and NCAA rules. In pro ball, the play described is a touchdown because nobody from the other team downed the player who had initially seized the football on the ground. However, in the college ranks, once that player touched the turf as he recovered the ball, the play is, of course, blown dead. To keep the football alive, he would have had to scoop it up, not pounce on it.

(13) This is definitely a TD, the same as if a player had blocked then had scooped the football up on, say, the five-yard line, then romped into the end zone.

(14) A special rule, much like a ground rule in baseball, had to be devised early in the facility's existence. It indicated the down would be replayed, and the game clock would have to be reset if a football made contact with the video board. In 2010 the entire league adopted a somewhat broader rule that states that when a ball hits a video board, a guide wire or a sky cam, the play is blown dead, the game clock is reset to when the play began, and the down is replayed.

(15) The seldom-seen rule involved here states, "Whenever a team presents an apparent punting formation, defensive pass interference is not to be called for action on the end man on the line of scrimmage."

ANSWERS

Joseph White, AP sports writer, did a piece on the above (and other obscure) rules, pointing out, for example, that an NFL player may not signal for a fair catch with two hands—that one will cost a player five yards—nor can he call for a fair catch after the ball has made contact with the ground—also a five-yarder. He wrote that what may be the strangest rule is the one that allows a team trying to go for one or two points after a touchdown to score without having possession of the football. White indicated that if the snap from center got loose and rolled around "and then a defensive player intentionally kicks or knocks it out of his own end zone . . . the kicking team is awarded the extra point." Note that even if they were going for a two-point conversion, they would only be given one point for the defensive infraction.

(16) Liner provides the answer here: "Batting a ball in the end zone is a violation for which the penalty is a touchback. Receiving team's ball, first and 10 on the 20."

(17) The call here is simple. In order for any kickoff to be legal, the football must go at least ten yards. Also, in order for the kicking team to snatch up an onside kick, it has to go ten-plus yards *and* either hit the ground or touch someone on the receiving team. So, in your question, the kicking team is tagged with a five-yard penalty.

(18) The new rule that came along in 1965 prohibited such a return—once a fair catch was signaled, there could be no return under any circumstances.

(19) Liner said this question may be moot in that officials probably wouldn't rule the kick was intentional, "because then you're reading somebody's mind. Let's take for granted that you have an official who decided it was an intentional kick into the end zone, then illegally kicking the ball is a spot foul, a 15-yard penalty from the spot of the foul and a loss of down." In addition, the ball would have been dead the instant it was kicked.

In the 1997 Nebraska at Missouri game, the Tigers led by seven with 1:02 left on the clock. The Cornhuskers then marched to the Missouri twelve-yard line with seven seconds to go, enough time for a final pass. Scott Frost fired the ball to Shevin Wiggins, but as he went for the reception, he was hit and the football bounced off him. Falling backward, Wiggins desperately kicked the ball that deflected to teammate Matt Davison who secured it with a shoestring grab in the end zone. The rather questionable TD counted and Nebraska went on to win in overtime.

Some illegal kicking calls are clear-cut. Liner gave such an example: "The punter, on fourth down, runs beyond the line of scrimmage and kicks the ball. The minute he kicks that ball, it's dead."

(20) Liner said, "I don't think you'll get that [roughing] call. It has to do with the intensity of the act. It's a safety issue. If the guy's trying to avoid him and he barely touches him, I cannot see where that that's a safety issue. I mean, technically, you're not supposed to touch the punter. That's why, for a long time, they had the difference between 'running into' and 'roughing' [the kicker]."

Of course, having such a distinction often put refs in a tough spot. "It was subjective. Whatever the official did, he was going to be wrong." If he gave the fifteen-yard call, a coach would argue the contact didn't merit that severe a punishment; and "if you give him five, they'd say, 'Hell, no, you should've given 15.'

"Now it's either roughing the kicker or it's not. If you're going to call it, it's got to be 15; if you're going to call it, let's make it something, let's make it a safety issue. If it isn't a safety issue, if you don't put the punter in any kind of danger, then leave it alone—it's hardly a safety issue. That's a judgment call, but they do want the quarterbacks and the punters protected. If they get them, they want it called."

The same holds true with some of today's penalties such as face masking. No longer is there the option for refs to hand for a five- *or* a fifteen-yard penalty. "Everything [used to be] subjective. Now the face mask, you've got to make some movement of his head."

Ultimately, says Liner, those connected with the game often don't want to focus on the petty stuff such as aiding the runner or barely brushing a punter. "They want the big stuff. If it's a flagrant hit, something that could have injured him, they want that called; anything else, let it go."

He added that even now refs have to be careful about some rules involving subjectivity such as punters faking that they've been knocked down. Again, this is an instance of a judgment call.

(21) Liner explained, "It doesn't matter if you're blocked into him or not. It's your responsibility not to hit the kicker. Those guys are vulnerable; you put yourself in that position [to possibly get blocked into the punter]—you just cannot hit them."

(22) Liner stated that holders cannot be hit by defenders while the kicker "is in position to kick the ball, is in the act of kicking, or right after he has kicked"—they are protected. However, "if the holder starts to get up and starts to move, he's no longer a holder. If he starts to run or decides he's going to punt it or pass it, he's fair game." He is also a fair target if a defender is able to get to him before the kick, even if he is holding the ball. It's as if he is a ballcarrier at that point. "If he's got the ball, you can get him.

"It's the same thing for the place kicker. As long as he's in position to kick the ball, which is one or two yards to the other side of the holder, then he's still a kicker; once he leaves that position or that holder leaves that position, then he's no longer a kicker. Then all bets are off."

23 Yes. There is no penalty. Liner cautioned, though, "As long as *you* touched the ball—you don't even have to block it, just tip it, touch it, make enough noise where the referee can hear, or see the tip which changed the flight of the ball—then you hit him, you're fine.

"But if you [touch] the ball and your buddy hits him, that's a foul. The guy that tips the ball is the only guy that can hit the kicker."

24 The football is not dead simply because a defender touched it, no matter how the touching occurred. Liner explained that in order for it to be dead, the defender has to possess the football; otherwise, the receiving team "can reach down, pick it up, and run with it." There are only two things that result in the ball being dead. "Possession by one or the other team or if it's rolling along there and *nobody* attempts to possess the ball—they're just going to let it roll dead so when the official deems that it's lost its momentum, it's not going one way or another [although] it may still be twirling or twisting or spinning or whatever, but it's not going anywhere. If he wants to blow it dead, then the official can blow it dead."

Liner said that by the letter of the law, "a defender could briefly pin a rolling punt to the ground with his hand, and walk away from what he believed was a dead ball only to discover that the official did not rule it dead and the receiving team was in possession of the punt running the other way."

In a related scenario, Dohanos noted that if a man covering the punt touched the football before the return man had the chance to field the ball on the fly, a different call is in order. "You have interference with the opportunity to catch."

Such an act of "illegal touching" is improper whether a member from the kicking unit touched the ball on purpose or not. Liner said, "You put a flag down and no matter what else happens the receiving team can always come back to that spot and take the ball. Once the ball was kicked and crossed the neutral zone, they [the kicking team] have given up possession, so now it's the receiving team's ball."

If the return man still grabbed the ball and, say, fumbled it away, the penalty would wipe that turnover out. They would, in that instance, take possession of the football.

(25) The infraction here is the same as on the previous question—illegally touching the ball by the kicking team. Liner said the spot of the foul is where the ball was touched. Therefore, the receiving team can, at worst, take the ball at that location. On the other hand, if the receiving team managed to possess the ball after it was touched by a member of the kicking team and ran it back for a substantial gain, perhaps even a score, they could decline the penalty in this "win-win" situation.

26 No. In theory, a team can lateral the ball indefinitely. This question is under the "kicking" section of this book because of one of college football's most famous kickoff returns ever—a play in which there were *five* laterals.

Rivals California and Stanford met in their 1982 matchup; and Cardinal quarterback John Elway had just executed an eighty-yard drive that ended in an apparent game-winning field goal, putting Stanford up, 20–19.

Cal's Kevin Moen gobbled up a squib kick at around the Bears forty-four-yard line, then lateraled the ball to Richard Rodgers who soon tossed it to Dwight Garner. Cal knew that once they were stopped, the game would end. Thus, the "lateral the ball any time you're in trouble" tactic came into play. Garner, surrounded by three would-be tacklers, pitched the ball back to Rodgers.

At about this time, the Stanford band, convinced the victory was theirs, rushed into the end zone. The zany action continued, though, with Rodgers surrendering the ball to Mariet Ford. When he got into trouble, Ford wildly flipped the ball over his shoulder to Moen. Ford then collided with three Stanford players; and miraculously, Moen banged through part of the band that had, by then, trickled onto the field, then bulled into the end zone where he spiked the ball on the head of trombone player Gary Tyrrell to cap off the bizarre series of events—a runback that came to be known simply as the Play.

(27) Although the crossbar is situated at a height, ten feet, which makes it possible for some players to "goal tend" a field goal attempt, this act is illegal. Officials are instructed to award three points to the kicking team in such cases.

There is even an NFL rule stating a player is not permitted to run forward and leap in an obvious effort to block a field goal attempt, then land on top of another player "unless the leaping player was originally lined up within one yard of the line of scrimmage when the ball was snapped."

(28) Halloran, under recently drawn-up rules, called the kick no good, knowing that the ball had to be entirely "within the plane" of the uprights. Kicker Russell confessed that his boot "was close and could have been called either way." The Skins lost, 9–7.

The play was much like one that would occur the day after Christmas in 1965 during the NFL Western Conference playoffs. Green Bay kicker Don Chandler tried to erase the Colts' 10–7 lead with less than two minutes left in the game with a twenty-two-yard field goal. Everyone in attendance, even Chandler, knew the ball went wide of, and higher than, the uprights, but officials called the kick good. The next season saw some changes put into place: the uprights were lengthened to a minimum of twenty feet above the crossbar, and goalposts were painted a bright yellow.

ANSWERS

29 The television broadcasters for the Cal versus Oregon game explained that a kick described in your question, with Tavecchio resetting and waiting on the snap, would have been legal.

In that same contest, California, like several teams this season, was accused of faking injuries to slow down Oregon's high-octane offense. This time the allegations were proven. California defensive line coach Tosh Lupoi admitted he instructed nose tackle Aaron Tipoti to feign an injury. Wire service accounts of the incident reported that replays clearly showed Tipoti "standing up after a play one second then on the ground moments later grabbing his left leg." The punishment was not one doled out by refs, but Coach Lupoi was suspended for one game.

30 Initially the kick was ruled no good; but upon further review, the officials could clearly see the football did break the plane of the goalpost, so it was indeed good. Dawson kicked a much easier one from thirty-three yards out in overtime to nail the win.

31 A rule stipulates that in such situations the ball cannot be advanced by the kicking team. Give the football to the Steelers at the twenty-three-yard line where Gay first took hold of the ball and strip the six points off the board.

Due to Pittsburgh's tough-as-steel defense, the Chargers got off only one snap from center all quarter long (versus twenty-four for the

123

Steelers)—and that play was a pass that was picked off. Now that's futility—one play for one pick over a fifteen-minute period. They seemingly would have done better fielding a team of eleven waterboys.

(32) Television announcers clarified the situation, saying once Bolden went out of bounds, he would not be eligible to recover the football. The ball went to the Vols.

(33) Dohanos said such a call is at the referee's discretion. "He looks around, and if he sees nobody's attempting to pick up the ball or is even coming toward the ball, then he blows it dead." Usually, he stated, it would be a matter of seconds. "It's a very short period of time."

(34) If a third-down field goal that is blocked is recovered behind the line of scrimmage, the kicking team, said Dohanos, "gets another down, but if [the ball] goes beyond the line of scrimmage then they cannot get a replay—it's over, you gave up the ball. Once it goes beyond the line of scrimmage you no longer have possession rights to it."

Dohanos further stated that "a field goal is treated the same as a punt in all enforcements."

(35) The flag flew immediately and, predictably, tussles broke out between the teams in the end zone. It was a ten-yard penalty for unnecessary roughness, but Harris was not ejected. Ultimately, the Cowboys got destroyed, 33–10.

MISCELLANEOUS SITUATIONS AND TRICK PLAYS

(1) When a delay of game penalty is called on the offense and the ref clicks on his microphone to announce who the guilty party was on the infraction, whom does he call the delay on?

Answer on page 165

(2) Then who is called for the delay of game penalty on a field goal attempt?

Answer on page 165

(3) The 2009 edition of the Backyard Brawl, a rivalry between Pitt and West Virginia that dates back to 1895, was held at Mountaineer Field just after Thanksgiving. WVU lined up in a formation that featured three receivers split wide, all three a yard or more behind the line of scrimmage, along with the quarterback operating out of the shotgun and a running back behind him. This is an illegal formation. Why?

Answer on page 165

ELI MANNING

4 As an NFL referee, how many seconds do you allot to a team before throwing your penalty marker and step off five yards for a delay of game infraction?

Answer on page 165

5 When eleventh-ranked Miami played host to the Florida A & M Rattlers on October 11, 2009, in Miami's Land Shark Stadium, the underdog Rattlers were trailing so badly (by three touchdowns) they tried to load up their defense against the Hurricanes by sending not the usual number of men, the legal eleven players, onto the field. No, they didn't attempt to sneak *one* extra man out there—they attempted to line up with *13* men on the gridiron! Alert refs caught this and made two defenders vacate the field. Just four plays later, the Canes rammed the ball into the end zone for yet another score. They sailed to a 46–16 win. Your question: what is the penalty in the above situation labeled, and how many yards get accessed for the violation of this rule?

Answer on page 165

6 In NCAA basketball action back in 1993, Michigan's Chris Webber became a figure of infamy when he signaled for a time-out when his Wolverines had none left. There the penalty was a technical foul that put North Carolina at the foul line and also gave them the basketball after that.

What happens in college football when a team that is devoid of time-outs makes the same mistake as Webber's?

Answer on page 168

(7) Another easy one for veteran fans. Notre Dame is a team rich in traditions and other things associated with their football program, including the Touchdown Jesus mural that peers down on the football field from its perch on a side of the Hesburgh Library, their leprechaun mascot, on hand in an official capacity since 1965, their marvelous fight song, the Golden Dome, and the line "Win one for the Gipper."

They were at home playing Washington on October 3, 2009, and led, 9–7, on three field goals with 4:51 remaining in the first half. Facing a third-down and seven-yards-to-go situation, Jimmy Clausen, Notre Dame's quarterback and one of three brothers who played quarterback in the college ranks (older brothers Rick and Casey did so at Tennessee), faded back to pass, trying to set up a screen pass to running back Armando Allen. However, a defender legally impeded the intended receiver, hanging him up so the play never developed correctly. Clausen released the ball from his own twenty-one-yard line, throwing it almost directly straight across the field, toward the sidelines. Actually, the ball was thrown just slightly behind where he was standing at the time of the pass—so the ball landed on the turf at the twenty-yard line. What was the call by the officials on this play?

Answer on page 169

8 In Pittsburgh on January 18, 2009, the Steelers met the Baltimore Ravens in the American Football Conference title game. In the first quarter, on the team's third possession, Pittsburgh's quarterback Ben Roethlisberger looked to pad his 3–0 lead. He spotted Santonio Holmes near the goal line and hit him with a strike.

In the process of being tackled, Holmes put one hand to the turf to help him leapfrog into the end zone. Extending his other hand, the one with the ball in it, he reached for pay dirt; and as he hit the ground, the ball came loose. The initial decision called for the ball to be placed at the one-yard line, causing Holmes, convinced the ball had hit on the goal line, to fume, and causing Pittsburgh's coach Mike Tomlin to challenge the ruling.

On the other side of the field, the Ravens weren't so sure what they had seen was, in fact, a legal catch. After some quick consideration, Baltimore head coach John Harbaugh also challenged the call. Can both coaches do this, or is the first challenge the only one that counts?

Answer on page 170

9 In the September 5 season opener of their 2009 season, the twentieth-ranked Brigham Young Cougars traveled to Arlington, Texas, where they were the guests of the number-four Oklahoma Sooners in a contest played at Cowboys Stadium. The favorite Sooners led 7–0 late in the second quarter when, on a first-and-ten play, Oklahoma

129

star quarterback and 2008 Heisman Trophy winner Sam Bradford threw a quick pass to wide receiver Ryan Broyles who was immediately wrapped up by Andrew Rich. An instant later, as Broyles was twisting toward the turf, Jordan Pendleton put a hit on Broyles, who was by then in the act of falling down. In fact, his knee rested on Rich, who was lying on his back, down on the playing surface. At that point, the contact with Pendleton appeared to cause a fumble that was recovered by BYU's Brett Denney.

Now, the question is this: does the turnover count; or was Broyles, on top of a tackler who was on the ground, considered to be downed already?

Answer on page 170

(10) On October 3, 2009, fourteenth-ranked Georgia squared off against LSU, a team then ranked number four in the nation. One look at some of the cars in the Athens, Georgia, parking lot adorned with "Geaux Tigers" bumper stickers let a person know the Bulldogs' opponents that day.

One story about the devotion of LSU fans relates the time the Tigers came up with a key score versus Auburn in a 1988 home contest. The cheering was so loud it caused a twitching of a seismograph at the school's geology department.

Now, in the Georgia game, neither team had crossed the goal line for the first three quarters. Suddenly, like heavyweight fighters trading brutal punches, the teams swapped quick scores—twenty-seven total points went on the board in the final quarter, twenty over the last two minutes and fifty-three seconds. The Bulldogs took their first lead by a slim margin of 7–6 when they finally scored during the opening minute of the fourth quarter. LSU then fought back to forge ahead, 12–7, when they came up with a TD but failed to cash in on a two-point conversion attempt. Georgia believed they had to score a touchdown or they would lose. They scored.

It took a sixteen-yard pass from Joe Cox to A. J. Green with 1:09 left on the clock to overtake the Tigers, going up, 13–12 (they also failed on a two-point play). However, the turning point of the game came immediately after Green's score when he appeared to make a celebratory gesture toward the spectators.

Just what does happen when a penalty occurs because a team is excessively celebrating in end zone? What is the ruling?

Answer on page 171

(11) Here's a follow-up question: On the Georgia kickoff after the penalty to Green, the Bulldogs lined up with seven men to the left of the kicker and three to his right. What's wrong with this situation?

Answer on page 173

(12) The year is 1968 and Deacon Jones, Los Angeles Rams' massive defensive end who was also known as the Secretary of Defense,

popularized a move that was known as the head slap. It basically worked like this: at the snap of the ball, Jones, with the speed of electricity, bolted from his defensive end position and took a mighty swipe at the helmet of the offensive tackle across the line from him. His specific target was the ear hole of his opponent's helmet. The contact created a not-too-pleasant and nearly-disorienting ringing in the player's ear. Coupled with his overpowering strength and savvy, this move led to many a quarterback sack—in fact, Jones is credited with coining the term *sack*. Your question is this: can a college or pro player now legally employ the head slap?

Answer on page 174

(13) Can a coach be ejected from a game for unsportsmanlike conduct? Back on December 29, 1978, Woody Hayes, the legendary coach of the perennial powerhouse Ohio State Buckeyes and a man who posted 205 lifetime wins (against only 68 losses and 10 ties) and laid claim to 4 national titles for OSU, got into a cauldron of controversy.

Hayes was definitely old school and subscribed to the grind-'em-out style of football epitomized by that famous football quote, "Only three things can happen when you throw the ball, and two of them are bad."

During the Gator Bowl, his Buckeyes took on the Clemson Tigers. Late in the game, Clemson's nose guard Charlie Bauman picked off an Art Schlichter pass and eventually got knocked out of bounds on the Ohio State sideline. Hayes, livid over the circumstances and the imminent loss, threw a punch at Bauman.

What was Hayes's penalty—if you were the ref, what would you have done?

Answer on page 174

14 Notre Dame played the visiting University of Southern California squad for the 2009 game between these long-standing rivals on October 17 with the Trojans looking for their eighth consecutive victory against the Fighting Irish and their tenth straight win over a ranked opponent. The Irish came into the battle ranked number twenty-five while the USC squad was perched at number six in the rankings.

With the Trojans leading, 20–7, Notre Dame QB Jimmy Clausen was flushed out of the pocket, forced to scramble around his right end, with Everson Griffen of USC in torrid pursuit. Clausen was caught from behind by Griffen who then, quite properly, walked toward the USC bench, but then hoisted his arms, flexing his biceps. Now, was that demonstrative move enough to cause a ref to fling his flag and step off yardage against USC?

Answer on page 175

15 Mike Curtis, a.k.a. Mad Dog, was a six foot three, 232-pound linebacker out of Duke, hardly a football assembly line (though it played its first football game way back in 1888 and its home stadium—due to ramifications of the outbreak of World War II—was the only place to host a Rose Bowl outside of California), but what a product Curtis was. Over his career, spent mainly with the Colts, he made hundreds of tackles, many of them savage, but perhaps none as famous as one that didn't even count in the official stats.

In 1971 a fan leaped out of the stands and onto the playing field during a game between Baltimore and the Miami Dolphins. Perhaps fancying himself to be a running back, just moments before the teams were to break their huddles, the inebriated man raced out to the line of scrimmage where the ball sat. The fan seized the ball and began to run with it, but he didn't gain much yardage. An infuriated and offended Curtis burst from his huddle, took a few strides toward the man, then hit him high and hard, leveling him and causing the football to fly high into the air.

Curtis, simultaneously breathing fire and spewing spit (a rather contradictory act that was nevertheless nearly the norm for him on a gridiron), stood over the man for a moment as if defying him to get up, as if saying, "Go ahead, get up and just try and recover your 'fumble.'" Baltimore teammate Tom Matte knew the fan had made a mistake when he tried to, as Matte put it succinctly, "steal Mike's football."

Curtis's intensity was summed up by one of his famous quotes, "I like football because it's the only place you can hit people and get away with it." One writer said he obtained a picture of Curtis decking the drunken fan and was delighted when Curtis signed it, "Keep off my turf."

Bottom line: what action did the refs take against Curtis that day? Did they (a) penalize him, (b) kick him out of the contest, (c) both of the above, (d) none of the above?

Answer on page 176

(16) On September 10, 1978, in week 2 of the NFL schedule, the Oakland Raiders and the San Diego Chargers clashed in a game that featured a wild finish. With just ten seconds left in the contest, Oakland's superb southpaw quarterback Ken "the Snake" Stabler faded back from the line of scrimmage, located then at the fourteen-yard line, looking to score a much-needed touchdown; the Raiders were trailing, 20–14. Chargers defensive end Fred Dean roared after him and made contact with Stabler, who, in desperation and under pressure from other Chargers, heaved the ball forward, later saying, "I fumbled it on purpose." His running back, Pete Banaszak, batted the ball toward the end zone. Before it reached there, Oakland's tight end Dave Casper kicked the ball at around the five-yard line, then followed the football's path and leapt upon it in the end zone as the game clock expired. Is this a score?

Answer on page 177

17 Say the Chicago Bears are losing by six points but are on the march, striving to score before time runs out in the first half of their game against the Green Bay Packers. After a ten-yard run down to the Green Bay six-yard line, the Bears have just enough time to run one last play. They hand off to Matt Forte, who tries to wriggle his way through the line but fails as the clock runs out on the half. However, the Packers were guilty of being offside on the play. What happens in such cases?

Answer on page 178

18 Imagine Oakland Raiders' Fred Biletnikoff, the gluey-fingered receiver, catches a ball over the middle where he is wrapped up by Kansas City linebacker Bobby Bell. While the future Hall of Fame receiver is in Bell's grasp, struggling to lunge forward for an extra yard or so, he is pelted by multiple Chiefs tacklers, hitting him like so many snowballs, one after another in a staccato barrage of body parts. Is Kansas City guilty of a personal foul here?

Answer on page 179

19 If you were officiating an NCAA football game that was tied after regulation time had expired, you would toss a coin and then give what options to the team that won that coin toss?

Answer on page 179

20 What other special rules apply to overtime contests in college ball? List as many as you can.

Answer on page 179

21 Last NCAA OT item: what happens if, after the first overtime session, the teams are still tied? Does the team that started the first overtime period begin this one too? Do the teams still begin their drive from the twenty-five?

Answer on page 180

22 With time dwindling rapidly in the final quarter and with number-three Texas about to be stunned by twenty-second-ranked Nebraska on December 5, 2009, the Longhorns were struggling to overcome a 12–10 deficit. They had just one time-out left but believed they could still get off a final few plays.

On second down and twelve yards to go, the next play resulted in a loss of one yard and precious time off the clock.

Inexplicably, Texas let it continue to tick down, feeling (a bit greedily) they could get off a quick third-and-thirteen play from the Cornhuskers' twenty-nine-yard line before bringing in Hunter Lawrence to kick a potential game-winning field goal.

They didn't get off the play, though, until only seven seconds remained in the game. When Colt McCoy, working out of the shotgun, then rolled out to his right, time became a huge factor—it appeared as if the Longhorns' last-ditch opportunity to win was about to be snuffed out. Then, finally—*finally*—seeing no open receivers, McCoy dumped the ball out of bounds.

Now, your question is this: by the time the football hit the ground out of bounds, the clock displayed on the television screen showed no time remaining. If that clock was correct, if it was perfectly synchronized with the official clock, then the game is over, right? Or was the ball dead, and the clock stopped once the ball passed *over* the sidelines when it broke the plane from the playing field to the out-of-bounds territory?

Answer on page 180

23 Fifteenth-ranked Pittsburgh played the visiting Cincinnati Bearcats on the same day Texas squeaked out their win over Nebraska. Every Bearcat and Panther fan realized the Big East title and an automatic bowl bid were at stake in this one.

With the score tied at 38-all in the fourth period, and with less than four minutes to go, Cincinnati's defensive end Walter Stewart committed a costly penalty that nudged Pitt closer to a possible game-winning score. While blocking fullback Henry Hynoski, Stewart thrust upward and forced the helmet off Hynoski's head. What's this penalty known as, and how many yards are stepped off for this one?

Answer on page 182

24 On December 31, 2009, the Oklahoma Sooners topped Stanford, 31–27 in the Sun Bowl. Ryan Broyles set a record for that event by scoring three touchdowns on receptions, all from Landry Jones who accounted for 416 yards through the air on the day. Broyles also established a team record with his thirteen catches, good for 156 yards.

Still, it was his involvement on a punt play that earned him a spot in this book. Broyles hauled in the punt from Stanford at the same time that coverage man Johnson Bademosi, a human express train, flattened him, causing a fumble that the Cardinal recovered. Initially the refs threw the flag on Bademosi charging that he did not give Broyles room to make a catch. So normally the correct call is, in fact, to penalize the kicking team, but what vital factor caused the officiating crew to huddle and to eventually reverse the call here? Clue: it involved an action committed by a teammate of Broyles who was in the vicinity of the play.

Answer on page 183

25 The final game of the 2009 season for West Virginia, ranked number sixteen in the country going into the fray, took place when they tangled with unranked Florida State in the Gator Bowl on the first day of 2010 in Jacksonville, Florida. The game had a fabulous marquee billing and was fated to be a very emotional meeting because the Seminoles head coach, Bobby Bowden, was retiring after a long illustrious career. This bowl game was the 522nd game Bowden coached in his lifetime. Over that span, he had coached a grand total of 3,388 players. His curriculum vitae included a stint at, fittingly, WVU. It was as if Fate had been the schedule maker for this bowl bash.

In the third quarter, the Mountaineers had the football at their own forty-yard line when a strange play involving not one but two penalties took place. First there was face masking on Kendall Smith after West Virginia's Tavon Austin took a wide receiver screen pass from quarterback Geno Smith at about the thirty-seven-yard line a few moments after he had backpedaled from the line of scrimmage to make the catch. Austin slipped out of Smith's arms before Greg Reid rode him out of bounds, then shoved him after the play had already been blown dead.

The refs had to sort out the play that involved both face masking and unsportsmanlike conduct. Which penalty takes precedence, or do both count against Florida State?

Answer on page 183

26 On the day after Christmas in 2009, Pitt butted heads with North Carolina in the Meineke Car Care Bowl game. Pitt was driving against the Tar Heels in the opening quarter with the ball on the UNC twenty-six-yard line. Dion Lewis took a third down handoff; and the swift running back found a hole in the defense, which is all he usually needs to initiate a successful run, and chewed up some serious yardage.

The play looked good until its conclusion when Lewis reached the one-yard line and fumbled the football across the goal line after taking a jarring hit from E. J. Wilson who, carrying out some excellent pursuit, roamed all the way over to Lewis from across the opposite side of the field where he served as the Carolina defensive end.

The ball hit once in the end zone, then squirted out of bounds at the sideline of that zone. What's the ruling here?

Answer on page 185

27 On January 4, 2010, the Fiesta Bowl in Glendale, Arizona, pitted Boise State, ranked sixth in the polls, against third-ranked Texas Christian in what Andrew Bagnato of the Associated Press called a "duel of unbeaten BCS busters."

The game was knotted at ten points apiece when the TCU Horned Frogs forced Boise State into what was ostensibly a must-punt situation—fourth down and a long nine yards to go with about 9:47 left in the contest, certainly not a time to gamble.

The only thing is that the Broncos were willing to toss those dice. With the temerity of a riverboat gambler, they called for a fake punt. Their kicker, Kyle Brotzman, protected by two men positioned a short distance behind the line of scrimmage in the backfield, both of them lined up around ten yards in front of Brotzman, took the snap and lobbed a pass to Kyle Efaw, normally a tight end, but one of the two men who had been set up in the backfield on this play. Efaw had slipped out of the backfield, snared the ball, and scampered for thirty yards and, of course, a first down.

Your rather simple question is this: did the play stand or based upon what you just read, had Boise State done something illegal here?

Answer on page 186

(28) Here's another play that calls for you to decide if something illegal took place. It was on New Year's Day 2010 when Northwestern tried a gimmick play against Auburn in the Outback Bowl held in Tampa, Florida. On the final play of the game, at the end of overtime, the Wildcats sent their backup kicker, Steve Flaherty, into the game for what was apparently a field goal try to tie things up and force the contest into a second overtime period. Northwestern coach Pat Fitzgerald felt that because his first-string kicker, Stefan Demos, had been injured earlier in overtime, his best bet was to run a trick play in an effort to score a touchdown to put a win in the record books and to end the game right then and there. "We played for the win," he would later say. "Unfortunately we ended up a little bit short."

Here's exactly what transpired: Zeke Markshausen took a handoff from between the legs of the holder, Dan Persa, and tried to sweep around the right end, but he was stymied by tackler Neiko Thorpe, who stopped him at the two-yard line. The game ended with a 38 on the scoreboard for Auburn and a 35 spot there for Northwestern.

Your question (and it's a pretty routine one for most good fans of the game) is this: had the Wildcats scored on the play, would it have stood or had Northwestern done anything improper on the play as described here?

Answer on page 187

(29) Almost exactly one month after Christmas 2008, the Indianapolis Colts received a wonderful present, an NFC championship. Under head coach Jim Caldwell, just the fifth rookie coach to make it to the Super Bowl, the Colts handled the New York Jets rather easily. It didn't hurt that Peyton Manning was on his game, clicking on twenty-six of thirty-nine passes for 377 yards, which made him the first quarterback in NFL annals to chalk up seven three-hundred-yard passing games in postseason play.

During the first drive of the second quarter by Indianapolis, Manning planned on running a quarterback sneak, which was, according to the Associated Press, "a play the Colts almost never ran." At that moment, the referee "stood over the ball for few extra seconds." What's so unusual about this?

Answer on page 187

(30) The 2009 season featured the Minnesota Vikings battling the New Orleans Saints from the Superdome (which, not long ago, was "a squalid refuge after Katrina") in the Big Easy for the right to advance to the Super Bowl. The exciting game went down to the wire; and because it went into overtime, you could figuratively say that it went *beyond* the wire.

Now, with the score tied at 28 apiece and only nineteen seconds remaining in regulation play, Minnesota, behind forty-year-old quarterback Bret Favre, was sitting pretty, having marched into field goal territory and in a first-and-ten situation with one time-out remaining.

They had spent their second time-out after they had advanced the football to the thirty-three-yard line, a position they felt was suitable enough to set up for a field goal try. However, the Vikings felt they had time to run another play and perhaps gain enough yardage to make the potential game-winning field goal more of a sure thing. They could then expend their final time-out, clinch the game with a kick, and gain the glory of a trip to Miami, Florida, for the Super Bowl looming two weeks away.

Coming out of the time-out, the Vikes huddled up. For some reason, Minnesota had twelve men in their midst. Is that a penalty that would be called right then and there, or is it one that would be called after they got off the next play?

Answer on page 187

31 In NFL action, Arizona was hosting Green Bay in the first round of playoff action on January 10, 2010, in a thrilling contest that was destined to go into overtime. When the game progressed to the second quarter, Arizona was in the lead, 17–0. The Packers were on the move, though, driving down to Arizona's forty-two-yard line and in a first-down situation when the lone setback, Ryan Grant, took a handoff from quarterback Aaron Rodgers. Grant swept to his right, got caught three yards behind the line of scrimmage, and was dragged to the ground by Gerald Hayes.

Because Hayes had his hand inside the jersey of Grant, he was called for a horse-collar tackle. However, the television announcers pointed out that Hayes did not actually yank Grant to the ground by his uniform and/or shoulder pads. Instead, approximately a few seconds after he had placed his right hand on Grant's shoulder inside his jersey, he used his other hand to grab Grant's thigh and make the tackle. Would that make any difference in the ref's call? Also, is this a five- or a fifteen-yard penalty?

Answer on page 189

32 Now a set of questions about NFL overtime games. Other than rules discussed earlier, what other special rules are established for NFL contests that go beyond regulation play? Clues: One rule deals with the amount of time-outs each team is awarded. Another part of this question requires you to explain the ruling concerning replays. Finally, what about the coin toss rule?

Answer on page 191

(33) The scene was Indianapolis, Indiana, and a trip to the AFC champion-ship game was at stake. On January 16, 2010, the Colts entertained the Baltimore Ravens in a game the Payton Manning–led Colts would eventually win, 20–3, outplaying the Ravens in the city which once housed the Colts all day long.

Manning was playing in his first game since capturing his unprecedented fourth NFL MVP trophy, and Indianapolis was playing at full strength for the first time in weeks. After they had built up a 14–0 win-loss mark, their coach, Jim Caldwell, rested many of his troops over their next two games, both losses; then the team had a bye because they possessed the league's best record.

The Colts' record coming off a week of inactivity in the playoffs had been 0–3 during the Manning Era; but after the victory over Baltimore, he commented, "This myth that you can't win after a bye week, I haven't believed in it."

At any rate, your call, and a ridiculously easy one for most fans, comes on this play. With a 17–3 lead in the third quarter, Manning went under center, took a snap, faded back, and fired a pass that was picked off by Ed Reed, good for his fourth career interception off Manning. Reed then streaked down the sideline some thirty-eight yards before the intended receiver on the play, Pierre Garcon, capped off his single-minded pursuit of Reed when he caught up with him and punched the football out of his grasp at about the twenty-eight-yard line.

The football stayed in play where Dallas Clark hopped on it, giving control of the ball back to the Colts. While the Colts lost some ground overall, the wild play still left them with a first down. They had also devoured priceless time off the clock, time the Ravens could ill afford to lose. But wait, was the knockout punch thrown by Garcon legal?

Answer on page 192

34 Chuck Bryant was a member of the Ohio State national championship team of 1961 and later went on to spend a season with the St. Louis Cardinals of the NFL before coaching high school football in Lorain, Ohio. Over the years he saw some interesting trick plays and formations—some legal, some not.

The Buckeyes had two special plays they called Ohio and Buckeye, depending upon if they'd run it to the right or left side of the field. "We would go up to the line of scrimmage and we would run off tackle plays—and remember, we were in two tight ends, a straight T [formation] in those days." After running the ball, say, to the right, Bryant, playing left end, would casually sneak across the field and line up on the right sideline. "There would actually be an unbalanced line. I would be up on the line of scrimmage, just standing next to the coaches, but I'd be on the field.

"We wouldn't go back into the huddle; we'd go to the line of scrimmage and the quarterback would just rise up and throw me the ball." Is this formation and, by extension, this play, legal? If so, would it still be a proper play today?

Answer on page 192

(35) Bryant ran some other trick plays as a high school coach. Would the following plays, covered over the next few questions, be legal on the college or pro levels nowadays?

"One play was called the 'Rosebud.' The other team would kick off and all of our backs [including the one with the ball] went into a huddle on about the 10-yard line and they all took off like they had the ball." The player who wound up with the ball ran for approximately fifty yards before being run down. "They didn't know where the ball was.

"We'd pick out a spot on the field," he continued. "If it was a middle kick, we went to one spot, if it was a kick to the right, we went to another spot, if it was a kick to the left, we went to another spot. About seven guys made the huddle and we always knew that the fastest guy was going to get the ball, so whoever caught the ball gave it to him." Then, everyone else "crossed their arms [as if carrying the ball tucked into their midsection] and took off in all directions. They didn't know who to tackle," Bryant chuckled.

He added that the remaining players not involved directly in the deception were "set up in a particular pattern so they were picking off [defenders] where we were going to run it."

Answer on page 193

(36) Bryant also employed a trick play he borrowed from another coach, one labeled Muddle Huddle. "We'd run a play then the whole line would go to the left except for the center and the quarterback and the tailback. The quarterback would throw the ball over the [confused] defense's heads to a halfback who was standing off to where all the linemen were and he'd run down the field with it." There are variations on how to run the play, but the keys are the formation, the confusion and element of surprise, and often a side snap by the center.

Bryant likened the play's formation to an extra point set up where "all the linemen are on the left hand side of the field. Well that's the Muddle Huddle, but you do it in the middle of the field and you take the ball—all the ball has to be is snapped, it doesn't have to be snapped between your legs—so sometimes the center just shovel passes it over to a back who's behind seven guys and they take off running. If the other team didn't adjust, they had seven on three."

He added that in his version of the play, an intended pass, if the defense smelled it coming, his linemen simply "shifted back and we had another play called." Plus, the odd formation could be used in other ways. "We could throw a screen pass, we could run it, we could hand it off, or the quarterback could run a sneak. We actually kept one guy over to the right of the center—in case you didn't cover him and went after the quarterback, we could throw a pass to him." It was a great play to catch the opponents off guard.

Answer on page 193

37 Bryant's next play also involved duplicity with some acting skills tossed in. "We lined up for a field goal and we put two guys to the left, on the wings, instead of one guy on each side. And our kicker would shout, 'Too many men on the field. Too many men.' So the second guy would run parallel to the line [to avoid an illegal motion call], we'd snap the ball, and throw it to him." The trickery here is the defense initially believes the man in motion is, in fact, simply running to get off the field before the team is called for the phantom "extra man" on the field. Legal?

Answer on page 193

38 Ohio State coach John Cooper tried an unusual play in the Sugar Bowl against Bobby Bowden's Florida State crew in 1998. Mike Liner, who worked that day as a line judge recalled that the Buckeyes faked a field goal when they "ran a receiver in off the sidelines and put him out there wide with Ohio State already in the field goal position, and they threw [to him] and they scored." Was it legal?

Answer on page 193

39 There was a play once that came to be dubbed "fumblerooski," a play run by, among other teams, Nebraska in the Orange Bowl of 1984. Down 17–0 to the Miami Hurricanes early in the second period of play, Cornhuskers coach Tom Osborne got creative. On this occasion, perhaps the most famous of all the times the play or a variation of it was called, quarterback Turner Gill took the snap from center then let the ball sort of drop, almost slide out of his hands and onto the ground near his right guard. At that point All-American guard Dean Steinkuhler scooped up the football, while Gill carried out a fake, acting as if he were running with the ball on a bootleg. The chicanery worked; Steinkuhler jaunted nineteen yards for Nebraska's first score of the day. Is this play legal?

Answer on page 194

40 On September 19, 2009, on the last play of the first half, Texas Tech's junior quarterback Taylor Potts had virtually no time (one second to be exact) left to get off a play—it was second down with one yard to go from his own thirty-eight-yard line—so he went behind his center, took the snap, then ended the play, ostensibly taking a knee. It appeared he was content to hit the locker room to regroup, trailing Texas, 10–3.

At least that's what everyone including the Texas defense thought. In reality, the QB faked touching the turf with a knee. What ruling would you make on this play?

Answer on page 195

41 The prototype for the prior question has to be Dan Marino's famed fake spike. On November 27, 1994, when his Miami Dolphins were trailing the New York Jets by three points, 24–21, with precious little time to play in the game, Marino and his coach, Don Shula, were desperate. Marino threw a completion down to the Jets' eight-yard line, setting up his ruse. He then rallied his team up to the line, giving every impression he was about to spike the ball in order to kill the clock at about the twenty-five-second mark. He even pointed to the turf and yelled out, "Clock! Clock! Clock!" to the officials to lend more authenticity to the gimmick play he was about to attempt. Everyone in the Meadowlands knew that a field goal would tie things up—of course, the Dolphins also were thinking that a touchdown would win this thing.

Then came the famous play. Marino found Mark Ingram for a touchdown. Was the play legal then? Is it still legal?

Answer on page 195

 42 The scene was the Silverdome at the start of an overtime game between Pittsburgh and Detroit on Thanksgiving Day 1998. Jerome Bettis of the Steelers came to midfield and, according to his account, called tails on the all-important coin toss prior to overtime play. The coin did land tails, but referee Phil Luckett claimed Bettis had called heads. What happened next?

Answer on page 196

43 Say the University of Hawaii breaks huddle and runs a play with only ten players on the field. What's your call?

Answer on page 197

44 Imagine the San Francisco 49ers are trying to ice place kicker Orlando Mare of the Seattle Seahawks. There are two seconds left in their game, and a field goal would win it for Seattle. The 49ers call for a time-out to make Mare think about his impending fifty-one-yard kick. Then, after the time-out and just before the snap of the ball, San Francisco calls for another time-out to really put the freeze on the kicker. Is there a problem here, and if so, what do you do to rectify it?

Answer on page 197

45 It was during a preseason game between the New England Patriots and the Oakland Raiders back in August 1978 when Raiders safety Jack "the Assassin" Tatum put one of the most violent hits ever on receiver Darryl Stingley. The collision broke Stingley's neck and left him a quadriplegic for the rest of his life. The helmet-to-helmet crash drew what penalty, and how many yards did the play cost Oakland?

Answer on page 198

46 In the BCS National Championship game held on January 7, 2010, between Texas and Alabama, a call had to be made on the first possession of the Longhorns.

Texas lined up in an illegal formation on first down from about the Alabama one-yard line, prompting the refs to toss a penalty marker on the field. After the play had been executed and the ball was dead, there was another infraction, unsportsmanlike conduct on the Alabama defense.

So what exactly takes place here? Are the penalties offsetting, or are both of them stepped off—five yards against Texas, then fifteen against the Crimson Tide?

Answer on page 200

 47 Who provides the game ball that is to be used in an NCAA game? Let's say a quarterback is very comfortable with the ball his team uses all week long in practice while the QB he's facing, from another college conference, is accustomed to another football. Must they both use the same ball during their game against one another, and if so, who gets his way, which ball will be in play; or are there other circumstances governing what football(s) are used?

Answer on page 200

48 Explain the penalty for "targeting" a defenseless player?

Answer on page 201

49 What do refs do when two players engage in a fight—say, they begin to tangle right after the play was ruled over? Do they penalize the man who provoked the fight, perhaps the one who threw the first punch; or do both combatants draw a penalty?

Answer on page 202

50 Say a player in college ball dives on a fumble and nobody else is around the ball for a second or so. Then there's a massive pileup. Can a ref not only say it's his ball right away, that he has obviously recovered the ball and the play is over immediately (because he made contact with the ground); but could the official even penalize others for jumping on top of the man who gained possession of the football?

Answer on page 203

51 What hand signal does an NFL referee give to indicate a time-out on the field?

Answer on page 204

52 Before the USC versus UCLA game in December 2008, the seventy-eighth time the rivals met, Coach Pete Carroll announced that his Trojans would don their traditional cardinal-red home jerseys at the Rose Bowl despite an NCAA rule mandating all visiting teams wear white. What punishment would he incur for the violation?

Answer on page 204

53 In 1976 the Bears lost a touchdown in an unusual way during a game against the Raiders. Oakland quarterback Ken Stabler fumbled early in the fourth quarter when Wally Chambers jarred the ball loose, and Chicago's defensive end Roger Stillwell was there to gather it in and carry the ball thirty-nine yards into the end zone. During Stillwell's run, twelve-year NFL official Chuck Heberling accidentally blew his whistle. What did the officials do in this situation?

Answer on page 206

(54) In November 2009, the outrageous Chad Ochocinco of the Bengals took a dollar bill onto the field while officials were reviewing a play involving a catch he had just made. While he did not extend the money to the ref as if offering a bribe, NFL executive Ray Anderson sent Ochocinco a letter in which he stated, "The very appearance of impropriety is not acceptable," and called Ochocinco's actions "unprofessional and unbecoming an NFL player." Your question is what did the refs do about such antics that day?

Answer on page 206

(55) West Virginia was on the road to play Rutgers for their final regular season game in 2009. A punt off the foot of Rutgers kicker Teddy Dellaganna was blocked by Kent Richardson, but the ball managed to bound seven yards beyond the line of scrimmage to the forty-yard line where it was scooped up by Jim Dumont of the Scarlet Knights. He protectively clutched the football to his chest and dashed twenty-five yards before he was brought down by Eddie Davis on a tackle that resembled a cowpoke rasslin' a steer to the ground. Why won't the Dumont advance of the football count?

Answer on page 206

MISCELLANEOUS SITUATIONS AND TRICK PLAYS

(56) When the Cleveland Browns faced the Buffalo Bills on October 11, 2009, an odd situation took place as the time left in the third quarter trickled down to about fifteen seconds. The Browns were in a punt situation but chose to let the clock run out so they could kick with the wind to start the final period of play. The Bills players, save one, saw what Cleveland was doing; so they left the field. At that point the Browns scurried to get off a play. Now, realizing their perilous plight, the Bills called for a time-out. Do you award it to them or not?

Answer on page 206

(57) Beginning in 2010, the NFL changed a rule involving a ballcarrier who loses his helmet during a play. Borrowing from the college ranks, what did the NFL come up with for such situations?

Answer on page 207

(58) Lately there have been quite a few football players whose hair extends well beyond the bottom of their helmets. That raises the next question: say safety Troy Polamalu intercepts a pass for the Pittsburgh Steelers against the Denver Broncos, and he begins to weave his way through would-be tacklers. Suddenly, in desperation, a Bronco reaches out, grabs a hunk of hair, and tugs Polamalu to the ground. Is this permitted, or will a penalty be called?

Answer on page 207

YOU'RE THE REF!

59 Conjuring up memories of the NFL playoff game of 1932 (mentioned in the introduction to this book), another notable football game also required some unique rules due to the event's venue. Like the '32 playoff contest, this one was also held in Chicago, but nearly eighty years later.

Wrigley Field, home of the Cubs, was the site of the Illinois versus Northwestern encounter of November 20, 2010. It was the first football game held there since the Bears played their final contest at Wrigley in 1970, and it marked the first college game there since DePaul held their home contests there way back in 1938.

Due to the cramped quarters, the field was laid out in such a way that the ivy-clad brick outfield wall in right field was situated just a few feet behind the east end zone. Although the wall was heavily padded, it still posed a peril for players. To remedy this problem, special rules were established. See if you can recall any of them.

Answer on page 207

60 In November of 2014 John Carroll University, the school that plays its home games in the stadium named after one of its most famous alumni, Don Shula, took on the University of Mt. Union in a battle of undefeated squads from the Ohio Athletic Conference, and a very obscure rule, just three years in existence, was the key to the game's outcome.

After Randy Greenwood pulled down a pass for a twenty-three-yard gain taking JCU down to the seven-yard line, quarterback Mark Myers was ready to take the snap from center with a mere two seconds left on the scoreboard. It was time for one last play, and if that play yielded a seven-yard touchdown the Blue Streaks would have completed a comeback from being down 24-7 at the half.

Now, with the score Mt. Union 31 and John Carroll 24, Myers, realizing he had no timeouts left, spiked the ball, doing so with about one tick left on the clock. However, what he did was not legal—why wasn't it?

Answer on page 208

(61) True or false: if a player grabs any opening on another player's helmet such as the ear hole or the back of the helmet and makes a twisting or yanking motion, that infraction is called "face masking."

Answer on page 209

(62) True or false: If a ball carrier's helmet comes off, the play is immediately whistled dead, but if any other player's helmet comes off during a play, no whistle is blown to stop the action—the ball remains alive.

Answer on page 209

(63) True or false: If a ball carrier's helmet comes off directly as a result of a face masking foul, he doesn't have to leave the game.

159

YOU'RE THE REF!

Answer on page 209

64 True or false: One rule change which was introduced in 2014 stated that in games where instant replay is not available to the officials, referees may review a first-half foul involving targeting during half-time when video is made available, and they may overturn their call and reinstate a player who was ejected from the game.

Answer on page 209

65 A defensive player makes forcible contact with the quarterback at or below his knee when the QB is in a passing posture. As a ref, do you: (a) ignore this, as the defender is simply going for a sack, (b) penalize him for going low and making contact with his shoulder, forearm, or helmet, (c) issue a warning to the defensive team, (d) issue a warning to both teams?

Answer on page 209

66 Teams such as Oregon are famous for their unusual and colorful uniforms. However, beginning in 2014 all NCAA teams were told their uniforms must display a contrast between their jerseys and the players' numerals on their shirts. True or false?

Answer on page 209

67 Another uniform question—what if a team comes onto the field pre-game with uniforms that don't display a contrast between the color of their jerseys and their numerals?

Answer on page 209

68 When Alabama played Auburn in November of 2014 in a wild affair 'Bama outslugged the Tigers, 55–44 to win the Iron Bowl. On a third down play with a bit under five minutes to go in the third quarter, and the score 33–27 in favor of the Tigers, both Crimson Tide receiver Quan Bray and Auburn's Bradley Sylve seemed to have equal possession of a pass from Nick Marshall as they fell out of bounds. The ruling was that Quay made the catch, and the gain stood.

The ball was spotted, ready for the next snap, and Auburn hurriedly ran a play before a review of the Bray catch could be considered or ordered. Can the refs ignore the subsequent play that had been run to its completion so they could review the previous play, or is this like a situation in baseball in which no appeal can be made if a pitch or play is made after, for example, a runner tagged up and possibly left third base on a fly ball before a catch was made?

Answer on page 210

69 In the NFL, are the following plays reviewable or not: (a) recovery of loose balls in or out of bounds (b) the touching of a forward pass by an ineligible receiver (c) an illegal forward pass beyond the line of scrimmage (d) checking to determine if a runner/receiver was in or out of bounds?

Answer on page 210

(70) Same basic question—are the following plays reviewable by NFL rules: (a) scoring plays, including if a runner broke the plane of the goal line (b) the forward progress of a player on any play not related to his making a first down or crossing the goal line (c) inadvertent whistle?

Answer on page 210

(71) On December 16, 2001, during the fourteenth week of the NFL season, the Cleveland Browns played the Jacksonville Jaguars, needing a win to keep their rather slim chances to make the playoff alive.

Jacksonville took a 15-10 lead on a field goal with 3:02 to go in the contest. The Browns moved the ball to Jacksonville's twelve-yard line with 1:08 to play, but were in a fourth-and-two situation. Tim Couch hit Quincy Morgan with a pass. Morgan secured the ball and held it close to his waist. It appeared that he took about two steps and then got drilled by James Boyd. As Morgan went down, the football came loose and bounced on the turf, but the refs let the catch stand and Cleveland gained three yards for a first down.

Shortly after that, the Browns spiked the ball, setting up a second down and goal from the nine-yard line. Referee Terry McAulay then acted, informing everyone that he would review the Morgan catch. Like an earlier item involving a college play, your question is this: was McAulay permitted to make such a call at this point, according to NFL rules?

Answer on page 210

TROY POLAMALU

ANSWERS

(1) The quarterback. Some fans might expect the center to be fingered for this penalty, but it's the job of the QB to trigger the play by calling for the snap.

(2) In this case, the holder is responsible as he, like a quarterback, is barking out the signal to receive the ball and to thereby start the play.

(3) The Mountaineers were penalized five yards because they had five men in the backfield.

(4) In the NFL, a team is permitted forty seconds between plays. That is to say, they have that much time from the end of a given play until they get off the snap for the next play to begin.

(5) It's called too many men on the field, although it is technically a form of delay of game, and it's a five-yard infraction.

Trivia item: in the 2004 NFL draft, the Miami Hurricanes set a record when six of their players went in the first round.

One of the most important plays involving the "too many men on the field" rule took place in the 1969 Orange Bowl between Penn State and Kansas. PSU was down 14–7 with scant time left in the

165

game, but they controlled the football. When quarterback Chuck Burkhart scored a TD with seconds left in the game, forty-two-year-old coach Joe Paterno told his troops to forget the tie—go for two points. When a pass to Bob Campbell, a wide receiver, was incomplete, the Kansas fans exploded out of the stands, rushing onto the field to celebrate.

That's when the officials took charge and pointed out that the Jayhawks were being penalized for too many men on the field. Later it was revealed that they had actually been playing with twelve men on that play *and* the previous three plays as well. After the penalty, Campbell ran with the ball, scooting around the left end to seal a 15–14 win.

Two more recent famous plays involving too many men on the field (or "illegal participation") came in 2010. The first time occurred when Tennessee and LSU met in Baton Rouge. With time running out in the contest and no time-outs left for LSU, the Tigers, down 14–10, hurried to get off a third down play; but confusion concerning the proper personnel to get on the field took over, and valuable time quickly slipped away. With the clock down to about one second, LSU got off a snap that went awry, apparently sealing the Vols' upset win—elated players off the Tennessee bench stormed onto the field.

However, Tennessee had experienced difficulty reacting to LSU's player changes, and therefore, the Vols had problems shuttling the players they wanted into the game. The refs detected thirteen defensive players on the field (three Tennessee players started to leave the field, four came in as replacements, and one man who had started off the field turned around and stayed in the contest). Given a reprieve, the Tigers scored on a Stevan Ridley one-yard rush and stayed unbeaten at 5–0.

Incredibly, the second time such widely chronicled chaos involving too many men on the field during the 2010 season took place also involved Tennessee. This time they were pitted against North Carolina in the Music City Bowl in Nashville. With time rapidly running out, the Tar Heels, down by three points, had the football and were within field goal range, but with no time-outs remaining. They ran a second-down play with sixteen seconds left in regulation. By the time the ref spotted the ball, allowing play to continue, there were only five seconds left. That is when the pandemonium broke loose.

As the clock ticked down to the zero mark, UNC was confused—some of their players were lining up to spike the ball, their only real play opportunity given the time factor, while other players from the field goal unit who had dashed onto the field seconds earlier were now trying to scurry back to the sidelines. Therefore, when T. J. Yates managed to spike the ball, his Tar Heels was guilty of having more than eleven players on the field.

After much review and confusion, North Carolina was penalized five yards and the game was permitted to continue; Yates was ruled to have successfully spiked the ball with one second remaining on the clock. Given life, and pushed back only the five yards, UNC was able to get organized and shuttle their field goal unit onto the field. Casey Barth then kicked a field goal to send the 20–20 contest into overtime.

In the second overtime period, Barth booted a twenty-three-yard field goal to finally end the game with a UNC 30–27 victory. Some fans felt Tennessee had been robbed and that UNC seemed to benefit by their own mistake. They pointed out that under NFL rules (specifically the ten-second runoff rule, a rule Vols coach Derek Dooley felt the college game "probably should get") the game would have ended and North Carolina would have lost.

6 "It's a delay of game call," said Liner. "Again, that's another stupid call—you try not to call it because that makes the coach look bad like they're not telling their kids what to do.

"I keep a card in my pocket, I know how many time-outs each side has because when it gets down late in the game the coaches are asking, 'How many have I got left?' We tell them. Keep in mind the scoreboards are unofficial so if it says two time-outs left on the scoreboard, coaches know that, they know the scoreboard guy may not be right.

"So, once one of the coach's kids runs up to me and says, 'Time-out, ref, time-out,' I'm going to try to ignore him; I'm going to get

ANSWERS

away from him. If he just stays after me, and the coach starts yelling for time-out, then I'm probably going to give him the time-out and penalize him.

"Sometimes they *want* that. That's the problem. You can't let them 'buy' a time-out for five yards. You can't let them do that—that's not fair. We try to ignore that call. That's why you don't ever see that called much." In fact, Liner said they might quickly march off the five yards, and "we'd start the clock immediately—it wouldn't be worth the time."

(7) Because the ball was thrown behind the quarterback's position, it is not a pass—it's a lateral. Furthermore, because the ball wasn't caught, it's now up for grabs. It was recovered by Washington Desmond Trufant, a freshman cornerback, at about the seventeen-yard line. From there, he scrambled into the end zone for six points on what counts as a fumble recovery.

Notre Dame eventually prevailed in overtime, 37–30, in a wild win over the Huskies. Clausen carved up the secondary, throwing for a staggering 422 yards, lifting Charlie Weis's Notre Dame squad to a 4–1 record at that point in the season.

In 2010 an interesting trick play involving a lateral took place when Presbyterian met Wake Forest, and three Demon Deacons figuratively sank into comas. The Presbyterian quarterback, Brandon Miley, intentionally skipped what must have appeared to the defense to be a short forward pass gone bad. The ball took a long hop off the artificial turf and into Derri Overholt's hands. It was a risky play they no doubt had worked on extensively; and it worked when the three defenders who were closing in for the tackle drew up short, and stared momentarily at Overholt who, ball in hand, acted as if the ball was dead. He then heaved the football to Michael Ruff for a sixty-eight-yard TD. In the end, though, Wake breezed with a 53–13 shel-lacking of Presbyterian.

The play, which some label Bounce Rooskie, dates back at least as far as 1982 when Nebraska ran it against Oklahoma.

8   Yes, both coaches can challenge a play. In this case, though, the officials ruled no legal catch had been made, meaning the appeal for a touchdown by the Steelers was a moot point. They declared the football had hit the ground before Holmes had firmly secured the ball.

9   The fumble call stood. If a man's knee(s), on top of another player or not, never touch the turf, and if no whistle is blown, the play is still alive.

Amazingly, throughout the entire 2008 season, the Oklahoma Sooners had fumbled just twice—they reached that mark on the Broyles turnover, matching the entire '08 total before the end of the first half of their initial game in '09.

ANSWERS

The Cougars went on to upset OSU, 14–13, in the first college contest and the first-ever regular season game held in the new $1.2 *billion* Cowboys Stadium. It was BYU's first win over a ranked noncon-ference team since they had knocked off top-ranked Miami back in 1990. The fact that Bradford sat out the second half certainly didn't help Oklahoma's chances. He had sprained his throwing shoulder when he was slammed to the ground on a clean play by linebacker Coleby Clawson late in the second quarter.

The next two weeks, Bradford was again on the sidelines. Remarkably, his backup, Landry Jones, did something on September 19 that no quarterback had ever achieved in the long Oklahoma Sooners football history—he threw for six touchdown passes! Jones, given his first name by his parents who admired legendary Dallas Cowboys head coach Tom Landry, connected on twenty-five of thirty-seven passes in an easy 45–0 drubbing of Tulsa.

Previously, Oklahoma QBs had thrown five TDs in a game on ten occasions, including five by Bradford, three by fellow Heisman Trophy winner Jason White, and two times by Josh Heupel, a Heisman runner-up.

(10) Well, refs certainly don't take away six points just because a team broke the rule regarding excessive celebration, nor is the offending team punished on the PAT. The penalty is simply accessed on the fol-lowing kickoff.

In our scenario, Green was flagged for a fifteen-yard illegal conduct penalty for his celebration even though wire reports later stated that "it appeared the player [Green] merely stumbled while trying to separate himself from the group [of celebrating teammates], which back judge Michael Watson interpreted as Green gesturing to the Sanford Stadium crowd—a no-no under college football's strict unsportsmanlike conduct rule."

After the call, it took just two plays for LSU to score when Charles Scott broke a tackle and sprang himself on a thirty-three-yard run with just forty-six seconds remaining. A two-point conversion ensued; and LSU wound up with a wild 20–13 victory, but not before a few more odd things had occurred (see next question).

Incidentally, a few days after the officials had thrown flags on Green like so much confetti on New Year's Eve, the Southeastern Conference verified what the media had reported was correct and announced that Green should not have been called for unsportsmanlike conduct.

Clearly such calls are highly subjective. Liner said, "The NCAA has just put so many things that are controversial off on the officials and things that should be taught by the schools and the coaches." That, he contends, is simple to do because officials are "easy targets."

That being the case, such calls can be difficult ones to make (although certain calling-attention-to-oneself actions such as diving into the end zone unnecessarily will trigger a flag every time). Liner stated, "Opinions are like noses—we've all got one and they're all different. You gotta' just hope that you've trained your officials to call the things that make sense. I mean, the guy who scores a winning touchdown, it's over—it's a dead ball foul anyway."

He continued, "There are two terms: one is called 'youthful exuberance' where a guy makes a great play, his team scores, or whatever, and you get excited and pat each other on the back—that's great. Now, if a guy's calling attention to himself [that's different]. The NCAA likes to view this as a team sport, so if a guy scores a touchdown, there were ten other guys that put him in the end zone—he didn't get there by himself. So they don't like that, anything that draws attention to oneself. Those are points of emphasis and they don't give you much leeway on these guys doing these orchestrated things in the end zone or standing over a quarterback after they've sacked him—there's not much room there in the NCAA. Now, in the NFL it's a different deal. I don't know how they put up with that. Some things they call, some things they don't."

(11) According to the rules, this formation is illegal. A team must have at least four men on each side of the football. Officials created the rule to prevent a team that is, say, about to make an onside kick, from stacking one side of the field with so much beef that an unprotected player on the receiving end might wind up the recipient of mayhem and/or injury.

LSU returned the kick and had an additional five yards tacked on to the runback due to Georgia's illegal formation.

By the way, when LSU then scored to win the game, they also, quite naturally, celebrated; and as was the case with Georgia a bit earlier in the game, their actions seemed tame. However, perhaps feeling a need to make up for the call on Green, the officials whistled LSU for excessive celebration. Just after Scott had scored what would prove to be the game-winning touchdown, he simply dropped the ball. It wasn't that clear-cut, though—he did stare up at the crowd and raised his arms, enough, the refs felt, to merit a fifteen-yard penalty on the following kickoff.

(12) While the play was legal in the NFL for quite some time, the league evaluated the dangers of the play—including possible diminished hearing on the part of offensive linemen who were getting cuffed by the paw of the ursine Jones, six foot five and 272 pounds, huge dimensions back in the day—and outlawed the maneuver in 1977. The head slap is also an NCAA no-no.

(13) No surprise here; the refs threw the penalty marker for his conduct and also threw Hayes out of the game, a 17–15 OSU defeat. However, his burst of anger proved more costly than that. The college decided they had had enough of the volatile sixty-five-year-old coach. Hayes was fired from Ohio State the following day, never again to coach at any level. One rash moment ended what had been a monumental career.

Hayes's blazing-hot temper and hatred of rival Michigan are well chronicled. A story, one which sounds apocryphal, claims he once ran out of gas in Michigan, not too far from the Ohio border. The curmudgeonly Hayes supposedly pushed his vehicle into Ohio rather than patronize a Michigan gas station. Another more plausible version of this story has Hayes's gas tank nearing empty while he was approaching, but not quite yet into, Ohio with Hayes steadfastly refusing to refuel while still in Michigan. "We'll push this [expletive] car to the Ohio line before I give this state one nickel of my money," he reportedly bellowed. And, in 1968, with a bulging 50–14 lead over the Wolverines, Hayes told his team to go for a rub-it-in two-point conversion. When asked why he had done this, Hayes defiantly replied, "Because they wouldn't let me go for three."

(14) The classic "look at my muscles" pose instantly drew a penalty for unsportsmanlike conduct. It is one of myriad celebratory moves that will cost a team fifteen yards for taunting. Most fans probably associate the penalty for gloating with players who have just scored a touch-down, but any player is susceptible to being flagged for such displays.

It was a foolish gesture by Griffen. His ostentatious display negated an otherwise fine defensive play. Instead of absorbing a sack for a loss, the Irish advanced the ball while being handed a first down.

Further, they went on from there to score on a strike from Clausen to the five foot eleven, 195-pound Golden Tate, the first TD pass surrendered by USC all season. That score cut the Trojans' lead to one touchdown.

Ultimately neither that score nor some heroics that took place later on a crisp drive engineered by Clausen mattered. USC won a 34–27 decision led by freshman quarterback Matt Barkley, a friend of Clausen's as well as a fellow southern Californian.

Of course, taunting in the NFL has taken on a one-upmanship theme. From the days of Billy "White Shoes" Johnson to the scripted antics of players such as Terrell Owens and Brent Celek who once scored a touchdown, then struck a pose much like that of the pirate displayed on the label of Captain Morgan's rum bottles, taunting and wild celebrations have grown and grown.

(15) Curtis received no punishment for his intervention that day. He later commented, quite simply, "He shouldn't have been out on the field." 'Nuff said.

Added info: the Colts gave a young Mike Curtis a look at the running back spot when he first came to camp, but he was so aggressive a move to the other side of the ball was in order. Teammates called Curtis crazy but single-minded in his love of contact and of football in general. For the record, Curtis carried the ball just six times in regular season play for one yard, an average of .2 per carry, about the same amount of yardage gained by the drunken interloper back in 1971.

Fans of the Pittsburgh Steelers liken Curtis's tackle to the time linebacker James Harrison slammed a Cleveland Browns fan to the turf during a game held on Christmas Eve in 2005. He pinned the man to the ground until security guards handcuffed the man and took him away. A teammate of Harrison, fellow linebacker Joey Porter, said if the NFL fined Harrison, he and other Steelers would pitch in and pay the fine.

16 The Chargers argued vehemently that there was no way this play, which came to be known as the Holy Roller, could be permitted to stand. However, referee Jerry Markbreit declared the play to be legal, and when Errol Mann's point after was good, the Raiders had pirated a victory.

If you missed this one, relying on your knowledge of today's rules, don't blame yourself—under the then-existing rules, the play was, in fact, legal. The rules makers huddled during the off-season and drew up new guidelines—to wit, any time after the two-minute warning has been issued, or when a fumble takes place on fourth down, only the player who has fumbled the football may advance it. If anyone else on the team that fumbles comes up with the ball, it must be returned to the spot of the fumble. There would be no more intentional "rolling" of the football for gain as the Raiders had done, holy or otherwise.

17 Neither the first nor the second half of the game can end on a penalty by the defense unless the offense declines that penalty, so the Bears would simply wait for the ref to step off half the distance to the goal and run another play of their choice.

A much-discussed play involving the rule about a half ending on a penalty occurred on December 6, 2009, in the Cowboys versus Giants contest at the Meadowlands. Dallas tackle Flozell Adams was flagged for a personal foul as time expired in the first half. The Cowboys had attempted and missed a fifty-seven-yard field goal. New York's return man Domenik Hixon caught the football and stepped out of bounds. Adams then shoved New York defensive end Justin Tuck from behind, earning an unsportsmanlike conduct penalty. Under the rules, the penalty was automatically declined.

The problem with that is it affords a team, in this case, Dallas, with the opportunity to take a free shot on an opponent. That's not to say a cheap shot artist wouldn't be ejected, fined, and/or suspended, but no penalty that could have a bearing on the game's outcome would take place. A suggestion was raised after the Adams incident calling for a penalty to be charged against the offending party on the opening kick of the second half. That rule came into effect in 2010 and also applies to penalties that occur at the end of the fourth quarter of games, which then head into overtime.

Recall that (as referenced on page 88) a new rule went into force in 2015 stating that if an *unsportsmanlike* penalty is called at the end of a half, it will carry over to either the second half or into overtime play.

There is no penalty against Kansas City, whose hits were clean, as long as they weren't hitting Biletnikoff after the whistle had blown—which wasn't the case here.

19 The winner of the coin toss can elect to start the first overtime period on offense, defense, or they may choose which end of the field to begin play in overtime.

20 Through 2010, college rules indicated that each team gets one possession per overtime period and starts their attack from the opponent's twenty-five-yard line. There is no game clock, just a play clock. Both teams are awarded one time-out per period. Furthermore, if things are still knotted in the third overtime period, teams are not permitted to kick the point after following a touchdown—they must go for two points. This rule is in effect to expedite the end of the game as two-pointers are, of course, more difficult to achieve than the chip shot of a kick.

In the NFL, new rules went into effect in 2010 regarding overtime play in the postseason. A team losing the coin toss is given one possession of the football if they should surrender a field goal, but not a touchdown, to their opponent during their first control of the ball in overtime. Previously, a field goal ended the game with the team that had just played defense going home a loser without a single touch in overtime. More on NFL overtime rules later.

Shortly after the 2010 rule change regarding overtime play in postseason games, another rule changed matters for all overtime games in the NFL. It meant that if the side receiving the football on the first kickoff in overtime scored a touchdown the game ended right there, as had been the case already. However, if they kicked a field goal, their opponent still got the ball. What was deemed fair and proper for postseason games became the standard for all overtime contests.

(21) While the teams involved in overtime play always begin their possession from the twenty-five-yard line, they alternate when it comes to which team begins a period with the ball.

(22) The clock does not stop until the ball hits the ground. Therefore, in this case—in the way the question was presented to you—the clock ran out and the game seemingly was over.

In reality, though, the television clock is neither official nor was it, in this contest, meshed perfectly with the game clock. Therefore, after further review, all of the Nebraska players and celebrants, who had stormed the field, had to curb their enthusiasm—the refs ruled there was one second left in this Big 12 championship affair.

Texas was to get one last shot to win the big one, remain undefeated, and move up a peg in the standings (because earlier in the day, number-one Florida had fallen to number-two Alabama, in a convincing 32–13 victory for the Crimson Tide).

ANSWERS

The media and many fans were perplexed as to why Texas had not expended their final time-out prior to their final pass attempt.

For the record, Lawrence—whose career-long field goal had been a forty-six-yarder and who had converted thirty-one of thirty-six of his lifetime field goal attempts (86% effective)—did kick a personal record-tying forty-six-yard field goal to pull off the narrow 13–12 victory, dashing Nebraska's hopes.

McCoy, under intense pressure all game, suffered through his most trying contest of the year (not completing his second pass of the night until well into the second half). Normally the All-American threw for a mile of yards; but in this struggle, neither team's miserly, unyielding defenses seemed to budge an inch. Nebraska could only earn five first downs and 106 yards (sixty-seven via the run and a nearly-invisible thirty-nine via the pass), their worst total in twenty-five seasons. Texas, with a BCS championship appearance at risk, could muster only a season-low 202 yards, 184 through the air and a meager 18 yards on the ground. McCoy was picked off three times; and he was sacked nine times, five times more than he had ever been nailed in a single game over his entire career. The normally staunch Texas offensive line became a sieve.

Still, Nebraska's defense wasn't quite enough to corral Texas as McCoy padded his win total, extending his record for being the winningest quarterback in NCAA history.

McCoy's lifetime record as a starting quarterback rose to 45–7 with just one game to go, the BCS National Championship game against Alabama in Pasadena. He would end up at 45–8, good for a .703 winning percentage while throwing for 13,253 yards.

(23) The official call was "hands to the face" according to the ref working the game. A television announcer noted that one can block near or at the throat, but any time a block gets up around the face, a fifteen-yarder is inevitable.

As an aside, on that play ballcarrier Dion Lewis, Pitt's freshman sensation who is astonishingly durable for a man who stands only five foot eight and checks in at 195 pounds, established a new single game school record by lugging the ball forty-three times, eclipsing the old mark set by Craig "Ironhead" Heyward.

Lewis, so elusive he darts around defenders like a dragonfly's erratic flight pattern, was en route to racking up the third highest total of yardage for a runner during the regular season—1,640, not to mention the extra 159 yards he tossed in during a bowl game at season's end which, at that point, propelled his total to the second best in the nation.

The eighteen-year-old sensation also became just the second player ever to be named the Big East Offensive Player of the Year *and* the Big East Rookie of the Year in the same season (the previous man to accomplish this was Michael Vick in 1999). And what a season it was—Lewis even topped "Touchdown" Tony Dorsett's freshman rushing record at Pitt by 113 yards. The old mark of 1,686 was set by

Dorsett way back in 1973 and was a record that remained standing for nearly forty years before Lewis came along.

Back to the game against Cincinnati: Lewis, with more swirling, dipping, spinning moves than the choreography of the Temptations while performing "My Girl," would cap off the Panthers scoring drive on his forty-seventh carry, scoring a TD, his third of the day, while shattering the old record for rushes in a game and lifting his ground yardage on the day to 194. He would go on to set a career high of 261 yards the very next year against the Bearcats.

However, the number-five-ranked Bearcats staged a dramatic late rally of their own to culminate a "barnburner" 45–44 win, one that earned them the conference title and kept them undefeated on the season, capping a great 12–0 streak on the year.

(24) An Oklahoma player, Jonathan Nelson, blocked Bademosi into Broyles so that the contact made by Bademosi was not of his own doing. To penalize him for running into Broyles on a kick-catch interference call would not be within the rules, so the fumble call stood.

(25) Because the unsportsmanlike conduct call came as a dead ball foul, both penalties counted. The FSU misconduct was extremely costly as the refs first slapped on fifteen yards from the end of the run for the personal foul of face making, then pushed West Virginia half the distance closer to the goal from that spot due to the after-the-play

infraction. Therefore, the Mountaineers ran the next play from the Seminoles' thirteen-yard line, having gained eighteen yards on the profitable run and another ton of yards (twenty-nine in all) for the two violations.

Later Bowden's troops, spurred on in part by their desire to send their coach off with yet another victory—taking a "Win One for Bobby" attitude into the battle—went on to win his farewell appearance, 33–21.

For the record, Bowden's FSU squad ended the season at 7–6, good enough for him to notch his thirty-third consecutive winning season at the university. In a world where many men cannot hold down a coaching job at a given school for longer than a handful of years, Bowden lasted forever and won for what seemed like an eternity as well. The eighty-year-old coach finished his career with a crescendo, wrapping things up neatly with a record that proudly stood at 389–129–4, leaving the major college ranks with the second most victories of all time, trailing only Penn State's Joe Paterno who, just hours earlier in the day, had inched closer to the 400-win plateau when he nailed down his 394th career win (he would reach the 400 mark in November 2010).

Paterno's 394th win came in a 19–17 win over LSU in the Capitol One Bowl, which also gave him his record twenty-fourth bowl victory over his long and illustrious career. One reason Bowden trailed the octogenarian Paterno was that in head-to-head play, Penn State boasted a record of 7–1 versus Bowden.

As a side note, Paterno, the granddaddy of all collegiate coaches, began his career as an assistant at PSU in 1950, so the 2009 season marked his *sixtieth* year at the university, the longest run for a football coach at any university in the land. Not only that, the following season was his forty-fifth as the Nittany Lions head coach, almost exactly twice as many years as Virginia Tech's Frank Beamer, the coach with the second longest run at a major college.

Meanwhile, back to Bowden, this is a coach who had won twelve conference titles along with two national titles. His roots extended way back to 1959 when he coached for Samford. Additionally, one of the most glowing statistics about his career is that between 1987 and 2000, his team was in the top five of the final polls every single season.

His final game also featured a sense of football history and symmetry in that Bowden's win over West Virginia came at the expense of Mountaineers coach Bill Stewart, who had been a 177-pound freshman walk-on in 1970 for Bowden during his first year at the helm of WVU.

(26) The Lewis fumble resulted in the ball automatically going over to North Carolina. They took possession at their twenty-yard line; it's a touchback for the Tar Heels. Interestingly, on that play Lewis's gain was sufficient to give him 1,691 yards on the ground for the year, enough to break Tony Dorsett's Pitt record for the most yards rushing by a frosh. He would wind up with an average of 138.4 yards rushing per game, third best in the FBS.

(27) To determine if this play is proper or not, just imagine Brotzman was a quarterback lined up in a shotgun formation—which, in effect, is what he turned out to be here. Further imagine, Efaw is a running back because, again, based on his position in the backfield, for all intents and purposes that's what he was on this play.

So, yes, Efaw was an eligible receiver; and the risky gadget play, called for by gutsy coach Chris Petersen, ultimately led to a score that gave the Broncos the 17–10 lead, a lead that held up over the final 7:21 of the game. The victory made Boise State the second school ever to wind up a season with a sparkling 14–0 record—Ohio State also did this in 2002.

Earlier in the game, a Brotzman field goal had put the Horned Frogs down by ten points. Remarkably, that represented the deepest deficit they had faced all season long.

Petersen noted, "We knew it was going to be a hard-fought game. A play here, a play there can turn the tide . . . We were fortunate to pull it out." Fortunate, yes; but as he well knew, sometimes a key play, in this case a very bold yet calculating one, can make the difference. By the way, Petersen went on to capture the Paul "Bear" Bryant Award at season's end, marking the second time in four years that he won the honor, which goes to the best coach in the country.

(28) Faking a field goal is pretty standard stuff; and while the way Northwestern did it certainly qualifies as a trick play, it's certainly not illegal.

Coach Fitzgerald commented, "I've had it [the play] in my back pocket for four years, and people tell me I'm too conservative. So I said, 'What the heck. We're here to win, so let's go.' He added, "And I'd do it again."

(29) According to Manning, "Unless we make a substitution, he's not supposed to do that." The ref is not supposed to slow things down in such a situation. Again, in the long run it didn't matter—the Colts did go into their locker room down 17–13 at the half, and they went on to score seventeen unanswered points in the second half to cement a 30–17 victory.

(30) The refs immediately tossed the flag, called the penalty, and moved Minnesota back five yards, a costly amount of ground given the position and predicament the Vikings were in.

Things turned uglier when, from the thirty-eight-yard line, Favre rolled to his right, out of the pocket, pump-faked, then got picked off when, with fifteen seconds left in regulation, he threw across the grain of the field and into the canine teeth of the defense. Further, it seemed as if he could have regained at least as many yards as the Vikings had lost on the penalty had he ran full tilt instead of pulling

187

up to pass the ball. Even if he had run out of bounds, his team still had one time-out left to regroup.

Instead, his ill-fated decision to pass the ball led to the worst-case scenario with Tracy Porter coming up with the interception. It was the fifth Viking turnover of the game. That set the stage for the Saints to (a) first run out the clock, (b) then win the coin toss going into overtime, (c) and nail down the NFC title by promptly parading down the field under the direction of QB Drew Brees, then kicking a forty-yard field goal that was booted by Garrett Hartley. Final score: New Orleans, 31; Minnesota, 28.

It was a sloppy game featuring nine fumbles and two interceptions in all. Turnovers killed the Vikings who were looking for their first trip to the Super Bowl in thirty-three years; the team, at that point, had lost five consecutive NFC title contests.

Again, under a new rule installed for the 2010 season, the Vikes may not have lost the game. The change in the rule book states each team must be given a possession in playoff games, which go into overtime if the team that wins the coin toss kicks a field goal on their first series. Team owners felt the flip of the coin carried too much weight in determining the outcome of vital contests. Dating back to 1994, when kickoffs were pushed back to the thirty-yard line, teams that correctly called the toss won almost exactly 60% of regular season overtime games. Owners no longer liked the idea of playoff games possibly hinging on a flip of a coin.

The victory represented the Saints' first win (in only two tries) in the conference championship. New Orleans moved to 15–3 and would face the 16–2 Colts in the Super Bowl. The Saints and the entire city went wild when New Orleans clinched it all weeks later, giving a enormous boost to the city that had suffered so much at the hands of Hurricane Katrina.

(31) The fact that Hayes didn't actually make the tackle by collaring Grant to the ground didn't make a difference on this play; the refs did penalize him. However, the announcers pointed out that the pure definition of a horse-collar tackle states the runner must be brought to the ground *immediately* by the force of the illegal tackle, the yanking on the collar. The proof that supports the broadcasters' contention that the tackle in question was clean is the fact that after Hayes initially grabbed Grant, the runner continued to struggle forward for additional yardage, and by then, Hayes's right hand had slipped off Grant's jersey. Clearly then, he was not jerked to the turf, he was tackled low. This penalty results in fifteen yards being levied against the defense.

Incidentally, this was one of the most entertaining postseason games ever. The two teams combined for an astonishing 1,024 total yards of offense (531 by the Cardinals against a Packers defense that was ranked number two overall in the NFL) and an eye-popping sixty-two first downs. In addition, the teams' total passing yardage was a whopping 801. The final score read Arizona, 51, and Green Bay, 45, in the overtime affair, and the offense was so prevalent each team punted just once all day long. The combined point total of ninety-six eclipsed the old record (of ninety-five total points set by the Philadelphia Eagles and the Detroit Lions on December 30, 1995) for a playoff game. The combined thirteen touchdowns also set an NFL playoff high as was the case with the nine total TDs through the air. In fact, three receivers reached a hundred-plus yards in the game.

It's noteworthy that the Arizona point total of fifty-one was still far shy of the record for the most points plastered on the scoreboard by one team in playoff action—the Chicago Bears won their title game over Washington, 73–0.

A missed wedge shot of a field goal from thirty-four yards out by Arizona at the end of regulation play had sent the game into overtime with the score tied at 45 points apiece. Rodgers then was stripped of the ball by blitzing cornerback Michael Adams. Karlos Dansby seized the ball after it had bounced off Rodgers's foot and raced seventeen yards into the end zone with the winning tally.

In the end, Green Bay, the team with the least amount of turnovers in the NFL, a mere sixteen, lost due to their inability to protect the pigskin—they began the contest with two turnovers and lost the game on a fumble. Ironically, then, this high-scoring affair was determined not by offense but by the defense, as the reigning NFC champs went to 11–6 and advanced in postseason play.

The game was a statistician's dream. Kurt Warner of the Cardinals threw more TD passes, five, than incompletions—just four on the day. The victory raised Warner's record in playoff action to 9–3 as he went 29 of 33 for 379 yards with none picked off. Warner's three-hundred-plus-yard showing was his sixth in playoff games—only Peyton Manning and Joe Montana had ever accomplished this feat prior to Warner.

In the meantime, Rodgers, making his first postseason start, went 28 of 42 with a team postseason record of 422 yards (the former mark was only 332 yards set by Lynn Dickey in 1983 versus the Dallas Cowboys) and four scores despite the fact that all but two of his yards passing came after the first quarter had been completed. Twice Rodgers rallied his troops back from a twenty-one-point second-half deficit, a feat that wire reports noted had never been accomplished by Brett Favre in Packers' postseason action. Unfortunately for Green Bay, the fifty-one points they surrendered was also a team record for postseason play.

32 Each team begins the first overtime session with three time-outs. The coin toss that takes place after the clock has expired at the end of regulation play ultimately determines who gets the first possession of the ball in overtime. Last, all replays in overtime are initiated from the booth.

(33) Of course it is legal to try to cause a ballcarrier to fumble as described on this play. It is the inherent job of a ballcarrier to protect the ball. Opposing players may strike the football, yank on the ball, chop at it, jab or take an uppercut (as Garcon did) at the football, or grapple it away from a ballcarrier—in fact, just about anything short of rubbing the ball with grease to make it squirt loose, puncturing it to deflate then steal it, or poking at it with a stick is permitted in an effort to help obtain the football.

(34) The play was, says Bryant, and still is, legal. He added that the key was "the defense really didn't pay any attention because we were always double tight end with a T-formation. So they really didn't even look to the sideline because we were so tight [grouped toward the middle of the field]." He recalled running the play for huge gains against Michigan State and Iowa.

Because OSU head coach Woody Hayes, noted for his "three yards and a cloud of dust" offense, was conservative, such trick plays were rare. "That's about the only one that we ever did," said Bryant.

ANSWERS

(35) This play is still a legal one at any level. In fact, a college team used a similar play but with the sleight of hand going on in the backfield on a play run from scrimmage, not on a kickoff.

(36) This play is also as legal as it is clever—even today, even at higher levels of football.

(37) Yes, this play, said Bryant, was fine, but he also noted that with any such play, "You always alert the officials so they don't blow the call." Bryant added that as a high school coach he would, at the end of each day's practice session, have his squad work on trick plays. "We prepared every week for, maybe, two or three trick plays. Also it helped us in case somebody wanted to run that [trick play or plays] against us—we would know what to expect."

(38) Liner recalled that as the fake field goal unfolded, "Bowden was coming down the sideline screaming at me. A guy by the name of Carl Johnson, who is now the Vice President of Officiating in the NFL, was my head linesman that night and he put the flag down on Cooper and Cooper went ballistic. So we brought that little deal back and not only did they not get the touchdown, but they got penalized 15 yards for unsportsmanlike, trying the 'hideout' play."

Liner explained a stipulation that currently makes the running of such a trick play more difficult to attempt now than it had been at one time. "Sometime between the end of a play when the ball is whistled dead and the time that the referee marks it ready for play on the next down, all 11 men have to be inside the numbers [on the field]." He continued, "There's a rule in the book that says you cannot use the substitution process of substitution in a football game to be deceptive—I don't care what part of the substitution you're using, kicking team, receiving team, defense, offense, it doesn't matter—it's got to be clear cut. They got 11 [men], you got 11, you get everybody set, we snap the ball."

(39) This question was rather tricky in its wording—the play *was* legal at the time. In effect, it was a fumble recovery by the guard. While his score helped the Sooners gain some momentum, Miami went on to win, 31–30. It should be noted that this play has since been banned by the NCAA, shortly after the 1992 season. Earlier, in the 1960s, the NFL outlawed the play as being "deceiving," and in 2006 the National Federation of State High School Associations also did away with the gimmick play.

Three interesting notes courtesy of Wikipedia: (1) Nebraska had run the same play back in 1979—again, in a losing cause. (2) Miami "fell prey to the fumblerooski in a national championship game a second time, in 1988." That time the Oklahoma Sooners quarterback Chuck Thompson deposited the ball on the ground for guard Mark Hutson to pick up. He took off for a touchdown, but OSU lost anyway,

20–14. So while Miami got duped both times, they still prevailed. (3) Technically, the odd play is not illegal now if run properly in the NFL. Referee Jerry Markbreit stated it would be a proper play if, and only if, the quarterback puts the football on the ground behind him—an intentional forward fumble is improper, but not a "backward" fumble.

One website, bigrednetwork.com, states that the last time this play was run in college ball was on Halloween day in 1992 by Will Shields of Nebraska in a lopsided 52–7 win over Colorado; it worked for a first down.

(40) Potts was, of course, trying to decoy the defense into letting their guard down so he could then straighten up and hit a wide-open receiver for an easy score. However, the ruling in college ball is that if a player simulates touching his knee to the ground, it counts as if he actually was downed. The refs alertly, despite confusion on the part of some coaches and media members, called this one correctly, ruling the play dead.

(41) The Marino play was proper and is still legal. Miami had been down 17–0 at one point in the third quarter, but Marino revived the Dolphins who eventually wound up scoring twenty-two unanswered points to overcome a 24–6 deficit. Every point the Dolphins put on the board, all of them coming in the second half, came via a Marino pass (save two PATs by kicker Pete Stoyanovich) including a two-point conversion and four touchdown strikes to Ingram. The game marked Marino's twenty-ninth fourth-quarter comeback of his career.

Tim Millis, who began his officiating career in the late 1960s and eventually worked his way up to become an NFL field judge, spoke about the fakes involved in questions 40 and 41. He stated that in pro ball, just as in the college ranks, "A quarterback can't fake going to a knee; this rule exists to protect the quarterback. He can legally fake a spike." A defender should be alert to a fake spike and he can see the ball is still in a quarterback's hand; but on a fake taking of a knee, it would be almost impossible to determine if he had touched down or not so an aggressive defender would tee off on the QB. The ball would be declared dead on such a fake in the NFL just as it is in college football.

42 What happened next was this: the Lions got the ball, scored on Jason Hanson's fourth field goal of the day, and defeated the apoplectic Steelers—one pictures Pittsburgh head coach Bill Cowher spewing spit in this, the first of five straight losses that would drop his record to 7–9 on the year. Nothing was done to rectify the incredibly botched situation on such a routine task.

Luckett later explained that he heard Bettis call heads, then change it to tails. Simplified, NFL rules state that the first choice made was "not subject to change." Bettis vehemently called Luckett's contention a "bold-faced lie." A new rule came into effect stating that players must make their call before the toss takes place, not while the coin is in the air.

(43) There was a time when there would be no call. A team can, of course, be penalized for too many men on the field but, in earlier times, not for having too few—after all, why would a team intentionally want to play shorthanded?

It should be noted that if a team nowadays did play with, say, ten men, that *could* lead to a penalty. Liner stated, "If you had all of your linemen and only three men in the backfield, you've got a problem. It used to be the offense could play with ten men if you wanted to, but you had to have seven on the line."

(44) There is indeed a problem. Such tactics are not permitted—no NFL team can call successive time-outs on the same down. The penalty for attempting to do so is a fifteen-yard unsportsmanlike conduct call.

This is not the case, though, in college ball (although there once was a rule prohibiting this tactic). A coach there could, if he chose to do so for some reason, use all of his time-outs, taken one at a time, before the start of a single play. For example, in the 2010 season opener for Utah, their head coach Kyle Whittingham, nursing a 24–21 lead, called a time-out to try to ice Pitt's kicker Dan Hutchins. He was about to attempt a game-tying thirty-yard field goal with just enough time to get off a final play in regulation play. Whittingham waited until the very last second to call for his time-out. As a result, Pitt, unaware of the late call, went through with the kick, which would have been good.

Then, again just before the next kick attempt, Utah called for a time-out; and just as had happened moments earlier, Hutchins went through with the kick—this time it tailed wide to the left, leading the home crowd to celebrate prematurely.

Just prior to the actual (and *third*) field goal attempt, Whittingham once more stood near an official—this time in an attempt to make Pitt believe he was about to call yet another time-out. Though he did not call that time-out, he was, typically of many coaches, looking for any little psychological edge he could muster. This kick was good, and Utah was forced to wait until overtime to clinch their 27–24 upset victory over number 15 Pitt.

Utah's win at their Rice-Eccles Stadium gave them a Mountain West Conference record-tying eighteen straight home wins. After the game, Whittingham admitted that in retrospect, he felt that calling for the second time-out had been a mistake.

(45) The Tatum hit did not draw a flag. Back then, there was no penalty, per se, for helmet-to-helmet contact. In recent years, illegal hits, wrote AP writer Rachel Cohen, led to players either being fined or ejected. Then, in late October 2010, due to a rash of flagrant hits, including one that resulted in a $75,000 fine being imposed upon Pittsburgh's

James Harrison, the NFL toughened its stance, stating that violent conduct would result in suspensions.

As a matter of fact, Tatum was not fined or suspended. Even the Pats coach, Chuck Fairbanks, stated there was no infraction and that the play involved, under the rules of the day, a hard—*very* hard—but clean hit.

Tatum, out of Ohio State, earned his assassin reputation with his physical style of play, hitting and dishing out punishment more like a linebacker than a defensive back. In 2001 when Jim Tressel took over as the head coach of the Buckeyes, he quickly created the "Jack Tatum Hit of the Week" award to be presented for, as Bill Livingston of the *Plain Dealer* wrote, "the biggest collision delivered by a Buckeye."

Even in 2010 when all the fuss about helmet-to-helmet contact became a cause celebre, the issue was confusing to many fans. For example, when James Harrison smashed Cleveland's Josh Cribbs in a game that season, that play was not construed to be illegal. Ray Anderson, NFL executive vice president of football operations, explained that Cribbs was a runner and "was not defenseless under our rules. . . . He wasn't under the category of defenseless player per the rules. Exposed? Yeah, but he was a runner. Runners aren't protected from helmet-to-helmet hits under the current rules." Anderson further stated that even a quarterback out of the pocket is also a runner "and subject to the same rules."

46 The officials charged five yards against Texas that placed the ball around the Alabama six-yard line, then assessed the dead ball penalty against Alabama. In this case, because of the Longhorns' position on the field, the refs moved the ball half the distance to the goal to about the two-and-a-half-yard spot on the gridiron, not the full fifteen yards for the unsportsmanlike conduct.

Liner called it a "live ball, dead ball [situation]. Forget the dead ball foul for a minute and just think about a regular live ball foul.

"They accepted the penalty instead of the result of the play, so they replay the down." Then, when the ball was dead, having nothing to do with the play that was run, "you administer the dead ball foul."

47 Liner also fielded this one, "Every team uses a different ball, *every* team. They all use whatever ball they want to use, and on each side of the field there are two ball boys from each team. Each of them have two or three balls in a bag and you change the ball on plays that go out of bounds and most of the time outside the hash marks and on long pass plays. We change, not every down, but when it's convenient. And all change of possession balls come in from the line judge's side—you have two ball boys over there with the line judge at all times. The balls are all a little different, but the deal is they're all approved by the NCAA. There are five or six different brands and it's whatever the quarterback likes, that's what that team uses."

Of course the air pressure in all of the game balls must be within certain limits, and refs check the pressure as part of their pregame duties. In the NFL, for instance, the football must be inflated to within a range of twelve and a half to thirteen and a half pounds of pressure.

(48) Liner explained that this penalty occurs when, for example, a safety "hits a defenseless player—like when a pass is overthrown to a receiver and you hit him anyway, or you hit somebody that's clearly out of the play—the play is going the other way and you come up and [hit a player]. Even though it might otherwise be a legal hit, there's no call for it. It's unsportmanlike."

It's doubtful that a player would be ejected for that unless, say, the hit was "a striking foul. It's still a contact sport. Obviously we don't want to get people hurt; but on the other hand, there are a lot more legal hits going on than are illegal. You're being pretty objective as it is, calling something away from the ball. I mean, most officials are not looking for that. They're looking for that overthrowing the receiver, but somebody blocking somebody away from the ball? It would have to be a blindside or some kind of illegal block to get that call. We watch for the defenseless player, the holder, the kicker, the passer, and the receiver that's been overthrown." It's a more subjective call on other players.

49

Liner chuckled, "That's always a subjective call. Typically, you see it offset because you never see it all [the skirmish/fight]. So if you just get one guy—usually you see him, but he's just the second one [involved], he's usually retaliating from being hit. So it's just easier to call it on both of them and try to settle them down. That's just for 'unsportsmanlike,' a late hit after the play.

"You don't want to call it 'fighting,' because if a guy gets thrown out for fighting, he misses the next game. So we try not to make it a 'fighting' deal. We're not afraid to do it, but the guy has to have acted up two or three times during the game for us to call it 'fighting' because that's a big deal these days; they've made it a big deal.

"You just don't see it much anymore—most coaches will get control [of the situation]. You go over to the coach and say, 'Coach, you want us to call 'fighting' on this guy or you want to get him out and talk to him.' They'll bring him out.

"We try to use common sense; we're not like, 'I got you' kind of guys. We're not police officials out there trying to arrest somebody. We're trying to just let them play the game within the boundaries of the rules. It's always better to tell the coach that some kid is hot; he's about to start fighting, 'So get him out, Coach. Get him out and talk to him before we have to do it for you.' Most coaches appreciate the heck out of it." Naturally, they'd rather yank a player for a few downs than be hit with a penalty and/or lose a player due to an ejection.

Of course, technically, an official could penalize one player and not the other. Liner also noted, "A swing and a miss is grounds for an ejection. Now a swing and a hit is certainly an ejection. It could be called 'fighting' or you can call it 'unsportsmanlike.' We prefer to call it unsportsmanlike so he doesn't miss the next game."

It should also be noted that if an unsportsmanlike call is made on, say, a swing and a miss after the play had been blown dead, the play still counts.

50 Dohanos stated, "If he gains—we call it football movement—control of the ball and he's down on the ground in college, he's down." Usually no penalty is called for jumping on the player (within a short period of time) who has recovered the ball—such a call would require a blatant piling on by a man, or men, from the opposing team.

Now, in NFL action, when there's a huge pileup on a fumble, the refs have been trained to wait before indicating which team has recovered the football, usually after they've untangled the entire mess, and the mass of players involved. Dohanos elaborated, "That's true. Let's face it, things go on underneath that pile. The guy that probably had the ball and was legally down no longer ends up with the ball because somebody stronger than he gets the ball. The job of officials is to get to that pile as soon possible, start peeling people off of that pile, and declare who has the fumble."

Dohanos added that if he clearly saw who had the ball first, before the ensuing mountain of men hopped on that man, "Then I wouldn't hesitate—I'd blow it dead right now and point in the direction that we're going." He'd do that even if after the players were disengaged, another man had subsequently come up with the ball and produced it for the ref to see. "It doesn't make any difference. That happens a lot. They'll come out of there afterwards because somebody eases up after they're told, 'Hey, o.k. it's your ball, white ball,' and a guy in a black uniform is still pulling [on it] and he picks it up and starts running. Looks real good, but he didn't get the ball."

(51) His hands will be crisscrossed above his head. If it's a referee's time-out, he gives the same signal, then places one hand on top of his cap.

(52) Carroll knew what the consequences for his action would be but didn't care that officials, under the Pac-10's way of dealing with the infraction, would strip his team of a time-out at the beginning of the game for the wearing of their home colors; he simply accepted the punishment.

UCLA empathized with their "crosstown" rival and declared they would purposely call an unnecessary time-out, burning it in sympathy, as soon as the Trojans were penalized. Carroll and UCLA coach Rick Neuheisel agreed about the importance of tradition and writers recalled the 1982 clash when both teams were decked out in their home outfits. Back then both schools shared the Los Angeles Coliseum.

Carroll insisted he didn't care about losing the time-out. "I think it's the fun thing to do, and I think the fans will appreciate it over time."

So moments after USC's David Buehler kicked off to open the game, referee Brian O'Cain clicked on his microphone and informed the crowd that USC indeed was guilty of "failure to wear required equipment," and penalized the visiting Trojans. When he also announced that UCLA was using a time-out, the crowd broke into an enthusiastic roar.

For the record, this rule was subsequently changed; and under certain circumstances (such as when the colors involved are sufficiently contrasting so as to avoid confusion), two competing teams can both wear colored jerseys.

By the way, if Penn State is Linebacker U, then USC has earned the title of Tailback U. Entering the 2010 season, a Trojan runner had reached a thousand-plus yards in a season on twenty-six occasions. The thousand-yard rushers include luminaries such as Mike Garrett, Ricky Bell, O. J. Simpson, Anthony Davis, Charles White, Marcus Allen, Reggie Bush, and most recently, Joe McKnight. In fact, Allen's 2,342-yard rushing on an incredible 403 carries in 1981 ranked number one in college football history at the time and made him the first college runner with 2,000-plus yards as well as the first college player to ramble for five straight 200-yard games at the start of a season, giving him 1,000 plus yards at a very early date. Further, in 2005 both Bush and running mate LenDale White hit the 1,000-yard plateau, combining for 3,042 yards on the ground.

53 Had the play been allowed to stand, the fumble runback would have stood up as the game-winning score, but this is a case of an "inadvertent whistle." Heberling told *Pro Football Weekly*, "I blew it when I shouldn't have, so the only thing I could do was give Chicago the ball, and that's what I did." The ball was automatically dead following the blowing of the whistle.

54 The pseudo-bribe cost Ochocinco nothing on the field, no penalty, but the league subsequently fined him $20,000.

55 The Dumont run doesn't count because the ball made it past the line of scrimmage. The Mountaineers took over at the forty-yard line. Now, if the ball hadn't gone beyond that line, then a run with the ball would have been permissible.

Trivia item: Rutgers, billed as the birthplace of collegiate football, began their football program (and played in college's first game ever—even though the sport then was in many ways more like rugby than the sport we now know) on November 6, 1869, with a 6–4 victory over Princeton. They have also been playing the sport for more consecutive years than any other college team.

56 Yes, despite the Buffalo oversight, they are entitled to call a time-out, one that certainly saved them a touchdown. Cleveland coach Eric Mangini said he wanted his team to "Snap it. And go," but he supposed his squad was taken aback by the situation and perhaps was under the assumption "that the official had stopped things." Just one man stood between the Browns and a score. "I was and I think 50,000 other people were screaming." Mangini's wish, he stated, was "go, block up the one guy, go, go."

57 The officials immediately stop play once the helmet comes off the ballcarrier's head, and the football is placed at what is known as the progress spot where the helmet became dislodged.

58 It is perfectly legal to yank on any player's hair. It was, after all, that man's choice to let his hair grow so long. As Dohanos put it, "There's nothing that says you can't grab any part of his anatomy other than the helmet."

By the way, in August 2010 Polamalu's hair, then almost three feet in length, was insured for $1 million by Head and Shoulders shampoo, a product endorsed by the Steelers star. They obtained the policy from the famous Lloyd's of London.

59 Actually, one could say the game was played under special rules; or as Big Ten Commissioner Jim Delany put it, the NCAA waived some of its regular rules "in the interest of student-athlete safety."

Here are some of the rules, including the two most important ones that required every single offensive play be run toward the safer, roomier west end zone: (1) All kickoffs were booted toward the east end zone. (2) After each change of possession, the refs repositioned the ball so the team on offense was headed for the west end zone. (3) Illinois used the "west team bench" for the first half, then switched with Northwestern for the second half, but both teams shared the same sideline (on the north side of the field).

The switch was made so that each team had the opportunity of being close to the all-important west end zone. Sharing the same sideline posed a problem when it came to making substitutions and it led to tight conditions for both squads, but Illinois head coach Ron Zook commented that his team had "worked all week about how there were 70 guys on the sideline, and we needed everybody to cooperate."

When the Bears played in Wrigley Field, the gridiron was laid out north–south, but even then, the confines weren't too friendly to football players.

The game itself featured Mikel Leshoure running wild—his 330 yards (he romped for 156 of those yards in the first quarter alone) set a new Illinois single-game record and ranked fifth all-time for a Big Ten contest. The Fighting Illini won handily, 48–27, in a game that featured just one touchdown, an interception return by Northwestern, going into the east end zone.

60   The new rule alluded to, FR-48, Article 5, states that no team can spike the football to stop the clock when there are fewer than three seconds left in any given quarter. The game ended with the Division III Mt. Union Purple Raiders notching their ninth undefeated season in a row and their twenty-sixth conference title.

ANSWERS

(61) True. Naturally, the term "face masking" makes one think of that particular part of the helmet, and that is, in fact, the part of the helmet on which a player yanks most often and most noticeably. However, if any part of the helmet is jerked, grabbed, and so on, it's technically termed "face masking."

(62) True.

(63) True. Under those circumstances, he may stay in the game.

(64) True.

(65) This rule went into effect in 2014— the correct answer is b.

(66) True.

(67) Officials can notify the teams to change into suitable jerseys before the contest starts. If they don't do so, they are to be charged with a timeout. The officials are to repeat the notification to teams about their jersey infractions between each ensuing quarter. Furthermore, if the team doesn't change uniforms before another quarter begins, they are to be penalized once more—charged with a timeout. This means a disobedient team could squander four total timeouts. Hardly worth indulging in sartorial splendor, so to speak.

(68) In our case, the refs disregarded the fact that Auburn got a play off and ruled they were going to review the previous play in which they had ruled a catch had been made. Be aware, though, reports later suggested that a referee had indicated that the official in charge of reviewing plays had, in fact, sent word that the play was to be reviewed *before* the next snap took place.

Auburn was furious that the hurry-up play they executed in order to thwart a possible review didn't serve its purpose, but they soon were appeased. The catch stood, but the play Auburn quickly got off did not count.

(69) In each case, the answer is YES, the plays are reviewable.

(70) Situation "a" is reviewable, but the other two are not reviewable.

(71) The Browns argued that when a team runs a play subsequent to a play that is in question, it is too late to call for a review. However, the officiating crew reversed the call, ruling there was no catch, so the ball went over to the Jaguars. Now, while the Browns' contention is correct under the rules, the replay official in the booth said he had buzzed down to the field to notify everyone that the play was under scrutiny before the next snap. McAulay also stated that there had been communication problems.

Added question: due to the problems involved here, was it proper to review the play even after the spike, or was that still not the way things should have been done that day? In other words, was it proper for the refs to review the play—and in turn, were the Browns being punished for something over which they had no control? After all, they did hustle to the line and they did spike the ball, making a smart play.

Here's one way of looking at it—Browns receiver, Andre King, told the Cleveland *Plain Dealer* that the communications breakdown was irrelevant. "That's just like a coach holding a [challenge] flag and throwing it too late after we snap the ball. Once the ball is snapped, you can't go back. No matter what it is. We felt robbed . . ." Well, as can be expected, the ref's call stood.

As a sidelight, Browns fans went wild, throwing objects, mainly bottles onto the field. For the safety of the players, McAulay called the game with forty-eight seconds left. Yet another couple of related questions here: is that an allowable decision and did it stand? If not, just who did make the final call here?

Chaos ruled and more bottles flew as fearful players wondered how they could safely get off the field and make their way to the locker room. About twenty minutes after the play in question was over, players in various stages of undress learned that the NFL's office had called, instructing everyone that the game had to be concluded. The commissioner said no ref had the authority to call a game off, so the Jaguars starting offense and the Browns defense had to return to the field. Many fans had left the stadium (some of them tried to get back in), but remaining fans continued to rain bottles down.

Some of the players came onto the field with no pads and/or no shirt and/or no helmet just to run a play in which Jacksonville took a knee.

Incidentally, a new rule resulted from this play, but not a football rule. The Browns decided that from then on they would not serve any beverages with caps on them, and they ceased selling alcohol at the conclusion of the third quarter.

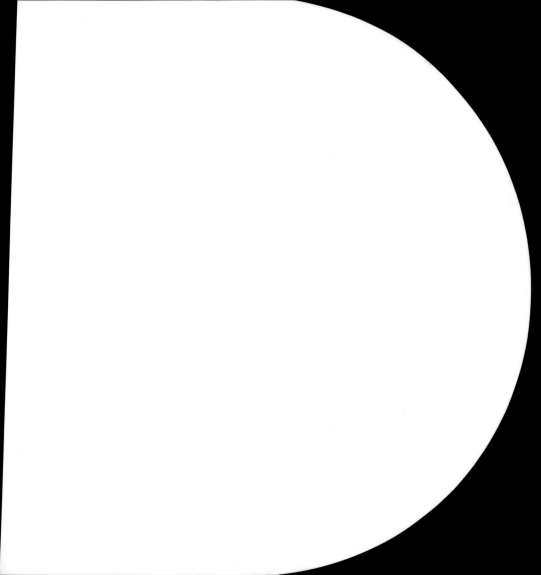

MARK SANCHEZ AND
LaDAINIAN TOMLINSON

THINGS YOU MAY NOT HAVE KNOWN ABOUT REFS

There can be no argument about it: football officials have an extremely difficult job. They have to deal with a constantly changing set of complex rules, some quite arcane, have to observe (and control) some of the strongest, quickest, and fastest athletes around, have to watch a mass of bodies in the trenches for sometimes nearly invisible infractions, have to make lightning-quick decisions with an expectation of 100% accuracy, have to stay in shape, have to endure draining travel as well as vitriolic abuse from fans, players, and coaches, and so on. Then after working a game, many refs have to report to their regular jobs the next day. Most fans are either not cognizant of or are unappreciative of what refs go through both physically and mentally.

Former NFL field judge Tim Millis, now the executive director of the NFL Referees Association, also held the position as the Big 12 supervisor of officials for ten years. He started a discussion of officials and their duties with one aspect of the job that many people don't know about, evaluation. "Every play [dating back for decades] in every NFL game is graded. The grades are provided to the officials; their ability to stay in the league as well as earning postseason assignments are based on these grades. Most colleges have a similar system now, but previously colleges' grading systems were not as detailed."

Millis also spoke of how refs are trained to do certain tasks on the field, things the average fan has no awareness of. "All the players on the field," he began, "are assigned to some official as an initial key, what we're to look at prior to the snap and right after the snap. So all 22 players are assigned to the seven officials. Therefore, the official is looking at more than one player."

Such a task, he said, may explain why a spectator might happen to notice "a guard flinch and the line judge doesn't see that false start—he may have missed that slight flinch [because] he may have been looking to see if the flanker has moved up, covering a tackle, making the formation illegal. People don't realize officials are looking at all the players and are assigned more than one player."

Of course, part of being an official is assisting other officials. If one official missed a call such as the guard flinching in the above scenario, another one would make the call if, as Millis said, "he feels it's solid. The calling official would get a 'correct' call, while the official who should have made the call would get an 'incorrect' no call because he should have seen this. If the grader can determine that the official was looking at something else legitimately—within his frame of keys—then he, of course, would just tell him he would not receive the 'no call,' but would be advised that he should have seen it."

One time Millis made a somewhat unorthodox move on the field that led to a correct call. In the grading system, he was rewarded for getting the call despite his leaving a position he normally manned.

"It was in the 1995 Indianapolis and Steelers championship game, the Hail Mary that [Jim] Harbaugh threw in the closing seconds of the game when they were behind by four points. The ball came down into the Colt receiver's chest. He reached with his right hand and turned and the ball touched the ground. We didn't have replay that year and I ruled it incomplete. TV showed the ball had touched the ground prior to possession of it.

"Without replay, if I make the wrong call, the wrong team goes to the Super Bowl. The unusual part of that play is that I actually left the sideline [his assigned area] as the ball came into the receiver; he jumped up and the ball hit him in the chest with three or four defenders around him; they start grabbing for the ball and he starts falling. I came into the field of play in the end zone to get a better view of the ball.

"The danger is, had that ball been tipped, knocked to the sideline, I wouldn't have been in the best position to make a call involving the sideline—clearly a case where I would have had to guess or someone [else] would have had to make the call. I came in because I wanted to make damn sure I watched that ball; and as he went down to the ground, had he just taken his left arm and put it up on the ball it would have been a touchdown, but he reached for it with his right hand and turned his body. The ball moved slightly and touched the ground. Of course he jumped up with it and showed it to me. I told him, 'No, the ball hit the ground.' He didn't argue!"

217

Millis had placed himself in a better spot than the area he normally covered in order to make this call. "At that time I had been officiating since the late sixties and after all those years of officiating at the high school, college, junior college, and professional levels, all of a sudden I become a recognized official with one call."

For the sake of reputation, future assignments, and survival, officials must be mindful of their grades. "The only security they've got is what the NFL Referees Association provides, and my job is to get the best working conditions for the guys—whether it's pay or pension or travel—and also to make sure that the grading system is fair and that it's administered correctly. For the most part if [an official] doesn't perform, he won't last!"

While each official's keys include certain players and specific areas of the field, the crew must work together and assist each other in certain situations. "Normally the calls are made by the officials initially assigned that area. For example, the back judge normally makes calls in the middle of the field. The field judge and side judge are on the sidelines. If the back judge can't see what happens, certainly the field judge or the side judge will call what he sees. Replay is available to correct an official's ruling in these and similar situations."

Then there's the catching process that Millis addressed. "Officials see hundreds of these—they go to training camp and just watch them over and over and over. The catching process on a sideline pass happens so quick that [one] would hardly think officials have time to do these three things, but they're watching the players—of course they're watching to see if there's any pass interference and if the receiver has stepped out of bounds, et cetera. Then they 'sense' the ball in. As an official, you kind of sense, and feel that the ball has now arrived, you immediately look down to the feet to see if they, in fact, come down in bounds. If they do, you go back up and make sure he has secured the ball. If he hasn't secured the ball, you've got to keep repeating the process. The process of ruling on sideline passes is completely backwards than what most people think. It's not ball and then feet, but it's feet and then ball.

"A unique part of being an official, that the public is unaware of, is the amount of time we spend studying on our own, and getting in physical shape. In addition to that, they have a four-day clinic where we concentrate on rules and mechanics. They also spend three to four days at teams' two-a-day training camps. Four or more officials are assigned to a camp to work the practices with the teams. They meet with the players, with the coaches as well as work those practices."

As for dealing with coaches, Millis said, "Officials aren't trained to be polite, nor should they appear rude or too authoritative. You just kind of talk to them firmly, but by the same token, your try not to be arbitrary or a smart aleck. If there is a problem, try to find the cause, stop it and move on. An official has to use preventive officiating in many of these type situations. If players are involved in pushing, shoving, taunting situations, the official tells the players and/or coach to stop the action or it will be stopped with a penalty. Normally they move on and the game continues."

Millis says officials tend to listen to complaints and tolerate them to a point. "As long as they don't get real personal with it and continue to harp on it, officials have to be somewhat deaf and just ignore most of it. If it gets to the point where they don't want to hear any more, they take the action to stop it. Most of it is just a real quick, angry outburst and the best thing to do is just keep moving, keep walking, and keep doing what you're supposed to do. The coach or player normally lets it drop.

"One of the best [approaches] I've found, on something I didn't call, is to tell the coach, 'You may be right. Maybe I didn't see it. You may be right, Coach. If I'd have seen what you just described, I would have called it.' To some extent you can kind of agree with him."

In addition, time allowing, a good official may explain why the coach is wrong, why he may be looking at a rule or play incorrectly. "I think good communications at the appropriate times, when the ball is dead, when you get a chance [is important]. Even if you don't have a chance, just say, 'Coach, I'll get back to you in a second,' and go back later and explain what you saw and what was ruled. *Most* of the time it pretty much levels off. He's not going to say, 'Well, thank you very much, I really appreciate that,' but at least he'll say, 'Yeah, well that is not what happened,' but he goes on, he starts coaching again and you start officiating again and that's what you want to happen."

Baseball may have patented the phrase "Kill the ump," but football coaches and fans are sometimes just as or more animated and acerbic than the managers and fans of baseball. However, clearly, refs *are* humans too and have feelings. In addition to wanting to avoid conflict, their human emotions show in other ways. For instance, getting to work the big game evokes feelings of pride and excitement for officials—once they get the job, that is.

Obtaining such postseason assignments is not easy. They are, first of all, based on the official's grades. The specific criteria have changed over the years under different supervisors or vice presidents of officiating. "It is always based on individual or crew grades, and there are stringent criteria for working the Super Bowl that go beyond working the normal playoff games. For example, an official has to have officiated five years and worked a number of other playoff games. There are special requirements for working any playoff game, but it goes a few steps further to work the championship games or the Super Bowl." A rookie ref, for example, no matter how skilled, is not eligible to work any playoff game; a second-year official could work a playoff game, but not a championship game or Super Bowl.

Super Bowl assignments clearly aren't made simply by drawing a name out of a hat. "Similar to the teams that are playing, these assignments are based on performance at the highest level during the season and a history of sustained acceptable performance by the officials. Most second or third year officials would be petrified, nervous or uncomfortable with a Super Bowl assignment. The tenure required, together with prior playoff experience and the present season's success, provide the necessary knowledge and confidence that allows officials to perform at an acceptable level in a Super Bowl."

The Super Bowl is so important that instead of having two alternate refs standing by, there are five. "The reasoning behind the five, which is something that's just been added during the last four or five years," said Millis, "is even though there are seven officials, there are five similar type positions— the line judge and head lineman have very similar positions on the field and very similar mechanics as do the side judge and field judge. So while they have different duties, they're still working the same space in the same type areas, so we have at every Super Bowl, an alternate umpire, referee, and back judge because their positions are different from any of the other ones. Then you have either, a line judge and a field judge, or you have a head linesman and a side judge.

"I can still remember the first one that I worked; and they [veteran officials] tell you, 'Don't be picky. Make sure that the fouls are there. These are the best two teams in the league.' I had [i.e., threw] a flag on the opening kickoff. After all the pre-game discussions, it never entered my mind not to throw it. I had a major face mask and I remember Jerry Markbreit, the referee, asking me, 'Is it five or fifteen?' Back then we had the five-yard and the fifteen-yard on face masking [depending upon the severity of the infraction]. I told him, 'Hell, Markbreit, I wouldn't have called it if it had been a five.' I would have passed on it on the opening kickoff."

Bottom line, Millis didn't feel as if he was under any extra extreme pressure or scrutiny. "Once the game kicked off, it was just a football game. There's no such thing as 'just *another* game,' it wasn't just another game—I've never had 'just another game,' but after the kickoff, it was a football game and you've got to do all the things in that game that you've done in every game you've ever officiated."

Nevertheless, he did say that, as he was "walking down the tunnel that day, the one thought I had that was probably different than I'd ever had was, 'You know, this makes all of those three-dollar Pee Wee games worthwhile.'

It's not that I didn't enjoy the Pee Wee games at the time, but you think of how many nights and weekend days you're away from your wife and kids.

"Some time during your football career, when you're gone three or four nights a week, you have to start wondering, 'Could I make more money working in a clothing store weekends? I wouldn't be away from the family.' But walking down the tunnel that day I thought, 'This *does* make it all worthwhile.' It does have a silver lining in the cloud. You don't do it for the money."

There's a line in *Death of a Salesman* about unsung people like Willy Loman deserving some attention. Likewise, respect, if not blatant attention, must be paid to football officials. As Millis concluded, "People don't really realize how much time they spend studying, talking, working out, pumping iron, running. The studying is year round; I really don't think I've ever met any official, at any level, who is not willing to spend some amount of time studying that rule book." Those who don't, believes Millis, won't last very long.

TODD HEAP

ACKNOWLEDGMENTS

Thanks to my informal coauthors on this book, my sons, Scott and Sean, who contributed greatly to this project. Thanks also to Rich Patch and Pete Carbonaro for their feedback and help.

Next, a big thank-you to my editor, Mark Weinstein, for all the help and advice he's given me over many years and many books (this is our seventh project together).

Many thanks also go out to Chuck Bryant, who played football for the Ohio State Buckeyes and the St. Louis Cardinals; Ed Dohanos, who has officiated football, basketball, and track at the high school and college levels and now works on the chain crew for the Cleveland Browns; Chuck Braun, who still officiates at a high school level after also working college games; Jon Kendle, a researcher at the Pro Football Hall of Fame; and especially to two former football officials for sharing so much of their time and expertise: Tim Millis, an NFL field judge who worked two Super Bowls, and Mike Liner, who spent thirty-five years as a line judge in the college ranks.

CAM NEWTON

ABOUT THE AUTHOR

Wayne Stewart was born and raised in Donora, Pennsylvania, a town that has produced a handful of big-league baseball players, including Stan Musial and the father-son Griffeys. As a matter of fact, Stewart was on the same Donora High School baseball team as Ken Griffey Sr. as a good-glove, no-stick bench player. Stewart now lives in Amherst, Ohio, with his wife, Nancy. They have two sons, Sean and Scott, and one grandchild, Nathan.

Stewart has covered the sports world since 1978 and has written thirty books to date and over five hundred articles for publications, such as *Baseball Digest, USA Today/Baseball Weekly, Boys' Life,* and Beckett Publications. Furthermore, Stewart has appeared as a baseball expert and historian on Cleveland's Fox 8 and on an ESPN Classic television show on Bob Feller.

MICHAEL VICK

SOURCES

Newspapers
Chronicle-Telegram
Pittsburgh Press
Plain Dealer

Magazines
Street & Smith's Official Yearbook Pro Football, 1979

Books
2010 Official Playing Rules of the National Football League (online document)
ESPN College Football Encyclopedia edited by Michael MacCambridge
Last Call by Jerry Markbreit and Alan Steinberg
Pro Football: The Early Years by David S. Neft, Richard M. Cohen, and Jordan A. Deutsch
Saturday's America by Dan Jenkins
The Scrapbook History of Pro Football by Richard M. Cohen, Jordan A. Deutsch, Roland T. Johnson, and David S. Neft
Sports Bloopers by Phyllis and Zander Hollander
The Sports Encyclopedia: Pro Football (7th edition) by David S. Neft and Richard M. Cohen
The Worst Call Ever! by Kyle Garlett and Patrick O'Neal

YOU'RE THE REF!

Websites

bigrednetwork.com

espn.com

foxnews.com

historyoffootball.net

hof.com

mikecurtisfootball.com

mmbolding.com

nfl.com

nj.com

nytimes.com

pittsburghlive.com

profootballhof.com

pro-football-reference.com

profootballtalk.nbcsports.com

quirkyresearch.blogspot.com

saturdaydownsouth.com

sports.yahoo.com

sun-sentinel.com

talk.baltimoresun.com

time.com

voices.washingtonpost.com

wikipedia.org

youtube.com

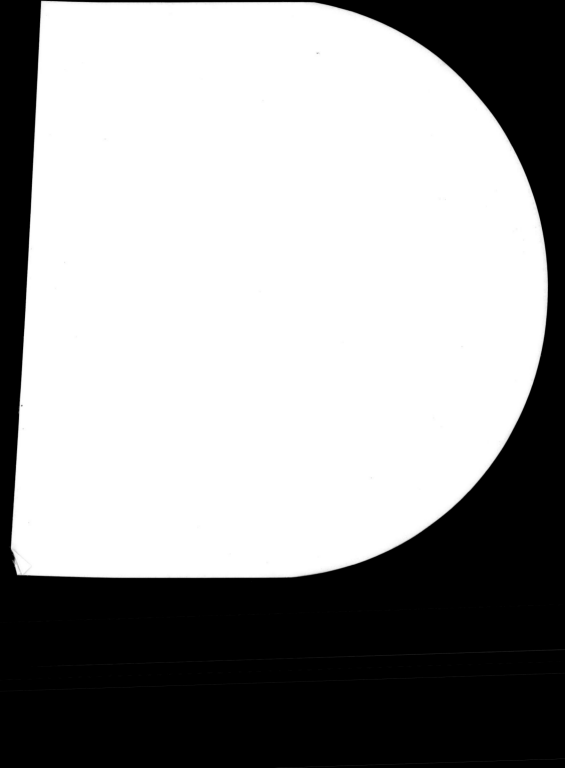

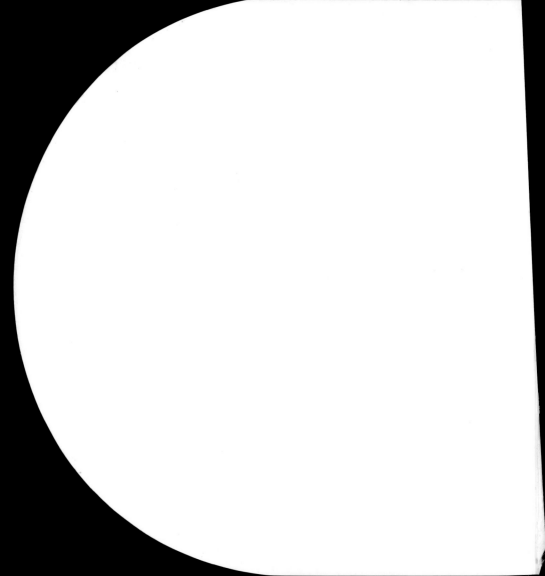